First published by The Word Bank in 2019.

Design:
a visual agency | avisualagency.com
Assistant: Lore Heyvaert
Typesetting: Main Point Books, Edinburgh.

Printing:
Pureprint

A catalogue record of this book is available from
the British Library. 9780993054419
ISBN : 978-0-9930544-7-1 | £15

ISBN 9780993054471

11500 >

9 780993 054471

THE
EVERGREEN

A NEW
SEASON
IN THE
NORTH

CONTENTS

Guest Editor: Lucy Ellmann
Contributing Editor: Elizabeth Elliott
Poetry Editors: Petra Reid, Jennie Renton
Editorial Goup: Hannah Bradley, Joyce Guthrie, Astrid Jaekel

The Word Bank is a community publishing collective run by Edinburgh Old Town Development Trust.

Edinburgh Old Town Development Trust is a Scottish charity (SC042964) committed to the revitalisation of the Old Town through stimulating growth in community participation, the arts and enterprise. It aims to support a vibrant, sustainable community in the Old Town by developing enterprising projects to meet local needs; establishing a network of gardens and green spaces; promoting education and training; and preserving the area's built and cultural heritage.

Acknowledgements:
Supported by Creative Scotland.

ALBA | CHRUTHACHAIL

INTELLECTUAL AND EMOTIONAL DIFFERENCES BETWEEN THE SEXES

.   .   .

WHAT WAS DECIDED AMONG THE PREHISTORIC **PROTOZOA** CANNOT BE ANNULLED BY ACT OF **PARLIAMENT**

PATRICK GEDDES AND J. ARTHUR THOMSON, THE EVOLUTION OF SEX, 1889.

In centring the voices of women, the fourth volume of *The Evergreen: A New Season in the North* offers a long-awaited reply to George Bannatyne, whose collection of poems and songs sparked the series of anthologies called Evergreen published by Allan Ramsay in the eighteenth century, Patrick Geddes in the nineteenth, and by The Word Bank today. Now one of the National Library of Scotland's treasures, the Bannatyne Manuscript is an imposing object, at 375 large leaves, all in Bannatyne's own handwriting. It opens with Bannatyne's plea for his 'reverend readers' to correct any errors they find in this book, made from his own old, mutilated copies of poems whose truth has stood the test of time. Bannatyne's book is framed as an endorsement of tradition, whose contents offer a moral lesson.

The respectable image Bannatyne cultivates in his opening poem is something of a pose, however. Bannatyne was twenty-three in 1568, when the collection was finished, and his claim – often doubted – that he wrote the book in three months, 'in tyme of pest', when 'we fra labor was compeld to rest' may have a defensive purpose, explaining how he came to have time to spend on a passion for music and poetry. Banntyne's manuscript is a young man's attempt to use taste to find a place for himself within his community. Yet, if Bannatyne is a little less pompous than he pretends, his collection is no more welcoming to women for all that.

Bannatyne's manuscript is a space where different currents of misogyny flow together. Some of the poems he collects reflect the influence of readers in holy orders on the literary landscape: satires on women validate the choices of those vowed to celibacy. Others are marked by humour at women's expense as a means to male bonding, teaching a particular kind of masculinity. As Carissa Harris argues in her pointedly-titled book, *Obscene Pedagogies*, 'Laughter becomes a litmus test for belonging among the "felawes": if one can laugh at women's sexual subordination and refuse to empathize with their trauma, then he is part of the group'.

Good women are present only in the form of Mary or the idealised beloved. Imperfect women are objects of revulsion, especially when they desire sex. In one poem, a squire reaching into his lover's petticoats finds that 'this mowth wald fane be fed'. For the squire, enthusiastic consent is a turn off: he makes his excuses and leaves her unsatisfied. Elsewhere, women are invoked in gross essentialist terms, as disembodied genitals: the proverbial thankless mouth. The poet prays 'god help and the haly rud /And keip all man ffra mowth thankless'.

Ramsay prints this poem in his *Ever Green*, along with others 'in derision of wanton women' or against laird's wives who

> ...give nae Budds,
> But on their Fudds
> They get grit Skuds,
> In nakit Bed.
> ...give no bribes,
> But on their hides
> Get good exercise,
> In naked bed.

Even in the hostile space of Bannatyne's manuscript, however, there are some pockets of resistance: the Wife of Auchtermuchty neatly foils her husband's plan to have her work in the fields while he takes over her work in the house. She manages his work well enough; he wrecks the place and promises to hold his tongue in future. Bannatyne also includes a poem by Christine de Pizan, often credited as the first woman to earn a living from her writing, and an advocate for women, though it's in Thomas Hoccleve's translation, and erroneously attributed to Chaucer.

Women's work is an unheralded presence in Ramsay's *Evergreen*, too: Ramsay's second volume ends with Hardyknute, apparently the fragment of an old ballad about a Scottish warrior. In typical style, Ramsay silently adds several stanzas of his own to this, and he was aware that this apparently ancient fragment was a much more recent poetic creation, by Elizabeth Halkett, Lady Wardlaw. Lady Wardlaw claimed to have recorded *Hardyknute* from the song of an old woman, but she was known as a poet in her own right. As Ramsay's son argues 'as this spectre of an old Woman had never appeared to anybody but herself, none of her acquaintance ever doubted of her being the true author'. Here, too, there are women's voices for those in the know.

Although Geddes' *Evergreen* had far more women amongst the writers and artists contributing to its pages, they remain a minority presence. Making up around a third of contributors, the most prominent and prolific of their number, Fiona Macleod, was the identity of another contributor, William Sharp. A closely guarded secret known to Geddes, for Sharp, Macleod was his 'truest self, the self who is below all other selves [...] my most intimate life and joys and sufferings, thoughts, emotions and dreams, *must* find expression, yet I cannot save in this hidden way'. The complexity of Macleod and Sharp's identity was not visible to the *Evergreen*'s original readers, nor is it fully legible to us at this distance and time, yet their dual presence within Geddes' collection underlines the fluidity and variety of gender within the Evergreen tradition.

Elizabeth Elliott
September, 2019

ZENO'S PARADOX

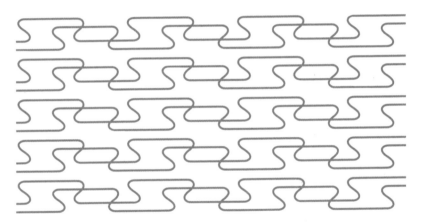

JUDITH HERTOG

Everything has fallen away. There are no sounds, no colours, no flavours, no scents, nothing to hold on to. I'm completely, utterly alone. The world dissolves, until nothing is left and I realise I'm at home, in bed, and Gil is asleep beside me.

Except for the sound of the heating system breathing hot air though the vents, the house is quiet. I lift my head and look around. A number glows in the dark: it's 4:10 am. The night-light in the children's bathroom throws a faint glow onto the walls of the hallway and reaches into our bedroom through the open door. I'm enclosed in a room, inside a house. Outside, across the country road that skirts our garden, the forest stands waiting to reclaim the land. The wall, so flimsy a blow can puncture it, separates our bedroom from the children's room, where Dina and Miki are asleep in their bunk beds. Sometimes I'm still surprised at how they appeared in my life. I nestle up to Gil. I want him to put his arms around me and reassure me I'm real. But when I press myself against his back, he grunts and moves away.

'Hot,' he murmurs in his sleep.

I chase him to his side of the bed and try to lock him in an embrace, but he remains elusive. The closer our bodies are together, the more sharply they seem to outline the space in between us; a space that can be halved, and halved again, and again... but I will never reach him.

Gil's skin is warm and sweaty. He may have a fever. I worry the incompatibility of our sleeping rhythms is making him ill. He is naturally a morning person – up at dawn and ready to go to sleep after dinner – but every evening I trick him into staying up late to keep me company. I'm afraid the effort is draining all his energy.

Last night, before he went to sleep, he complained of a headache, and I, immersed in a book and impatient with the interruption, told him to take an aspirin and said I'd join him when I'd finished my chapter. Of course I stayed up until I'd read the whole book, and when I finally went to bed, at one in the morning, I found Gil asleep with the lights still on. After all these years he still trusts me when I say I'll be there soon.

'You have to get up now!' Gil says, 'It's a quarter past seven! Dina and Miki will be late for school!' I try to open my eyes, but my lids are glued together.

Through my lashes I see him standing beside the bed, looking down at me. As he comes into focus, I realise the person I used to know has been transformed into a middle-aged college professor, his face thickened and set in lines of worry, fatigue and responsibility.

'I'll get up in five minutes,' I say, 'I just need to finish my dream.' I have used the same excuse every morning for years, and Gil has given up arguing. He complains that trying to get me out of bed tires him for the rest of the day.

If only I could split myself up so that I could keep on sleeping, while my alter ego goes through the morning routines. In my mind I make my alter ego get up, brush her teeth, comb her hair, get dressed, go to the kitchen to fix breakfast, make coffee – and just as I'm starting to feel pleased with her progress, Gil reenters the room.

'Why can't you just get up! Why do you do this every morning?' His voice rises in despair. I feel bad for the distress I'm causing, but my exhaustion is stronger than my sense of remorse. I close my eyes and burrow underneath the blanket. Tonight, I'll be better. Tonight, I won't keep him waiting. Tonight I will go to bed early.

'Just one more minute. It's not yet twenty past,' I mumble. Gil threatens to just leave and let me sleep. He says he doesn't care if I get fired; this is the last time he'll try to wake me up. From now on I'll have to take care of myself. But he has the same outburst every morning, and I know that his sense of responsibility is stronger than his frustration. I settle back under the blankets knowing he'll return in a minute. He stomps out of the room and tells Dina and Miki that they have to get dressed by themselves because Mama won't wake up. They mutter some kind of protest: they don't know what to put on because Mama hasn't laid out their clothes last night.

'Can I wear my princess dress?' asks Dina.

'No!' I want to shout. 'No! You can't go to school in a princess costume!'

'I don't care,' says Gil. 'Just get dressed!'

If I were a better mother, the sound of my children's voices would stir my maternal instincts and give my reluctant body the strength to get out of bed; if I were a better mother, I'd wake up long before my children stirred, just to stare lovingly at their slumbering faces and awaken them with kisses and songs; if I were a better mother we'd have breakfast together every morning and I'd drop Dina off early at school so that she'd have time to play outside with her friends until the bell rings. But I'm not a good mother. I have no idea what my children do in the mornings. I don't even know what time they wake up. All I know is that when I finally come into the kitchen, they are usually dressed and eating breakfast.

'It's seven thirty!' Gil shouts.

How nice it would be to lie here without anyone nagging me. How nice if the whole world just disappeared and I could sleep forever in this warm nest. What would happen to me if Gil gave up on me? Would I just sleep my life away? Would anything ever convince me to get up?

Gil's angry footsteps are coming down the hallway. That's it. I've pushed him too far. I jump out of bed, take one big step to the dressing table, grab my hairbrush, and position myself to make it look as if I've been standing there, brushing my hair, for at least five minutes. Gil knows my childish pretence but as long as it gets me out of bed, he puts up with it.

I inspect my closet in search of an outfit. Clothes tend to give me a sense of purpose. I'm no longer lost in dreams; I become a woman with a job, a style, and somewhere to go. But today nothing captures me. I have too many clothes, and almost all of them are impractical or inappropriate: 1950s vintage dresses, ball gowns, a Chinese qipao, a Bedouin dress with gold and purple embroidery, and a bunch of hand-down blouses from my mother. I grab my burgundy corduroy pants and black sweater from the laundry pile and pick a pair of pearl earrings.

It's a quarter to eight when I enter the kitchen.

'Finally,' says Gil, who is spreading peanut butter on Dina's lunch sandwich. Every day he prepares the same lunch for her: a sandwich, raisins, and apple slices, which Dina doesn't touch because they are discoloured by the time she unpacks them. Gil doesn't usually pick Dina up from school, so he doesn't know that most of her lunch ends up in the trash. If I made her lunch, I'd pack her different fresh fruits every day, cashew nuts, cheese, dates, yogurt – a perfectly balanced diet. But of course I'd have to get up in time.

I brush Dina's hair, my only remaining parental responsibility in the morning. Gil still hasn't learned how to handle her long curly hair. If he did, he'd stop waking me up.

Miki climbs out of his chair.

'I'm done,' he declares.

'No, you have to finish your yogurt!' I object, and as the words leave my mouth I have already given up. I can't make him eat if he doesn't want to.

Every morning two bowls of barely touched organic yogurt remain standing on the breakfast table. And every afternoon when I come home after picking up the children, I feel sad when I see the bowls with spoiled yogurt and soggy cereal still standing in the sink.

Gil is obsessed with the news. To him, turning on the radio is as essential as switching on the kitchen lights. He knows of every disaster, war, and massacre reported in the international news. I try not to be too aware of tragedies that don't directly affect me. The radio broadcasts a report about a bombing in Baghdad. A disturbingly upbeat voice announces that the death toll so far is thirty-eight, with many more people injured.

The voice explains that suicide bombers targeted a crowded shopping street. I turn off the radio.

Gil is already standing by the door. He tells Dina and Miki to put on their coats immediately because it's time to leave. I remind him I'll take Dina to school, that I'm not defaulting on my responsibility.

'It's five to eight. She's going to be late if you don't leave right now,' says Gil.

'But I *am* leaving now,' I object, 'I'm ready!' I glance at the wall clock. It's only 7:53, but I figure I can't start making myself a sandwich now. I'll just buy myself a coffee and a muffin in the coffee shop. If I had gotten up five minutes earlier, I could have made my own breakfast and donated all the money I waste on coffee and muffins to a good cause.

Miki is ready to go. He is standing by the door in his winter jacket and snow boots. I realise I haven't even talked to him this morning and won't see him again until I pick him up from daycare. I try to hug him tight to make up for the separation, but he pulls away and reaches for the doorknob. Gil sighs. Yes, I know. Dina will be late again for school.

'I'm sorry,' I apologise to Gil, 'I'm just so tired in the mornings.'

'Why don't you just go to bed earlier?' he says.

'I'll try,' I promise, knowing I won't.

I pucker my mouth for a kiss. Gil responds with a quick lukewarm touching of his lips to mine.

When we were first in love, almost twenty years ago, we couldn't have imagined ourselves like this. I remember us hiking in the mountains. (Back then Gil still humored me when I proposed hikes and other strenuous activities that didn't interest him.) The wild almond trees were blossoming and the ground was covered with fresh winter grass and splashes of red poppies and pink cyclamen. (Back then the almond trees always blossomed, the grass and the flowers shone with an almost unbearable brilliance, and I even seem to remember violin music playing softly in the background.) We had such an abundance of bliss, I couldn't imagine it to run out in a lifetime. We made love under the almond trees, on the living room floor, on a bench in the university's botanic garden, on the beach with the midday sun blistering Gil's back, and in my rented room while my crazy downstairs neighbour was screaming she'd set the house on fire. And each time I expected us to transcend the constraints of time, gravity, circumstance, and self – ultimately merging our souls into each other, like that perfect being described by Aristophanes in *Symposium* – the creature that results from the joining, in perfect love, of two people, and that, in Renaissance woodcuts, looks a bit like Humpty-Dumpty.

There was the promise that if we held on tight, we'd never again be lonely or afraid. But the longer we're together, the more our selves get in the way of our togetherness. This is what love has to offer now: the coordinating of our schedules so that the kids will be picked up in time from daycare and school; the managing of household chores; the daily irritations with each other's failings; the keeping score of each other's offences (Gil's irritability versus my irresponsibility; Gil's inability to keep the house clean versus my inability to wake up in the morning; Gil's incurring a twenty-dollar fine at the library versus my charring of the pumpkin soup); our constant gushing about the children's cuteness because we're too tired to think of anything more interesting to say to each other; and occasionally a rushed kiss or embrace to remind ourselves why we started on this project. Instead of transcending the limitations of our selves and our bodies, we've learned to live with each other's flaws in an equilibrium of irritations.

I grab Gil for another embrace, something more faithful to what we imagined ourselves to become when we made love under the almond blossoms. I pull him against me and tilt my head for a kiss. I know Gil doesn't like kissing – especially not when Dina and Miki are waiting by the door, already late for school – but I want to signal that I miss him, and that I still intend, one day, to catch up. Gil grudgingly kisses me back and we have a little tug of war as he tries to withdraw while I try to glue my lips to his.

WORLD OF
ILLUSIONS
CITY TOUR

ASTRID
JAEKEL

MIND THE GAP

A WORLD OF ILLUSIONS BECKONS

The 'World of Illusions City Tour' collage by Astrid Jaekel is a response to selected images of the Old Town detailed below from 'Photographs from the Survey of Edinburgh, c1904–1910', part of the Patrick Geddes Collection and used with the kind permission of University of Edinburgh Special Collections, with special thanks to Elaine McGillivray, Project Archivist.

p20
Waverley Station from West Signal Bridge

p28
From Canongate Churchyard – the old Royal High School is in the background. Panmure Close, Canongate. Text References: Robert Fergusson, Robert Burns and Adam Smith

p36
Dangerous playground South Gray's Close – St Anne's School playground. Tron Square – South part of Tron Square

p42
Candlemaker Row garden after completion – view of Cowgate and Central Library. Lawnmarket – Panorama of the Lawnmarket looking north. Text reference: Lewis Mumford

p52
Castle Esplanade from the Outlook Tower. From Married Quarters looking East – from Johnston Terrace. Text reference: Norah Geddes

p62
Main Point – at the west end of West Port, looking into High Riggs. Text reference: Lewis Mumford.

Selection of photographs and additional text by Joyce Guthrie.

PLAYING WITH HISTORY: GEDDES' MASQUES

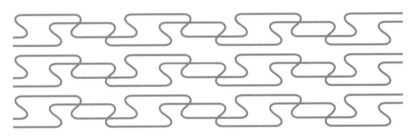

ELIZABETH ELLIOTT

23

In 1912, University Hall marked the twenty-fifth anniversary of its foundation with a remarkable piece of theatre, *The Masque of Learning and Its Many Meanings*. Staged in the Synod Hall with a cast of 650, the *Masque* reflected a contemporary vogue for large-scale historical drama known as 'pageant fever'. Later expanded into the *Masque of Ancient Learning* and the *Masque of Medieval and Modern Learning*, this masque was a small affair in comparison to events such as the 1907 Oxford Historical Pageant or the Scottish National Pageant of Allegory, Myth and History (Edinburgh, 1908), involving casts of thousands. Performances on this scale are necessarily collective endeavours, dependent on community involvement and support, for both players and spectators. This cooperation at the heart of pageantry fostered the belief that these events promoted collective identity and civic virtues.

The University Hall masques, like University Hall itself, were devised by Patrick Geddes. Like most pageants of this kind, the masques were visual and largely wordless spectacles, accompanied by a 'book of words' to help the audience follow the performance. Geddes' Masque Books were later republished as *Dramatisations of History* (1923), achieving a readership far beyond the original theatrical audience. Here, Geddes underlines his sense of the masques' social value: 'although University and City came in separately upon our stage, they go out together [...] instead of losing their individuality, they are creating the latest and greatest of faculties, that of Citizenship'.

At its root, modern pageantry was a conscious revival of the dramatic tradition of medieval mystery and miracle plays performed by town guilds, and stemmed directly from an 1899 masque produced by the Art Worker's Guild, *Beauty's Awakening*. Calling on the audience to remember how 'in past days...guilds of craft presented masque and show', the Art Worker's prologue made the connection: 'E'en so do we, a Guild of Arts, prepare /A mystery'. The medievalism of new pageantry appealed to conservative interests, adding to its enormous popularity, yet its beginnings reflect the Arts and Crafts movement's investment in the Middle Ages as a model for labour and social life. Medieval cycle plays often took place at the feast of Corpus Christi, commemorating Christ's body through a celebration of the social body, with citizens coming together to make these performances possible. Modern pageantry offered a similar form of communal performance, inviting spectators and players to experience the performance as a group, while the plays themselves reminded those involved of their shared history. The effects of this kind of theatre outlast the performance, transforming its participants by making them aware of their collective identity, both intellectually and as a bodily experience.

Geddes' players went on to form an association, the 'Edinburgh Masquers, Outlook Tower', the name underlining the sense in which the masque enacts the role Geddes envisaged for the Outlook Tower. The civic museum Geddes established at what is now the Camera Obscura in the 1890s was intended to offer an overview of the development of the human species. Storied exhibits, spiralling down in space and outwards in focus, moved from Edinburgh at the top, through Scotland, to the world, complementing the panoramic view of Edinburgh, which was used as a concentrated image of the historic development of a city. Writing on 'Edinburgh and its Region, Geographic and Historical' in 1902, Geddes argues that the historic centre was 'probably the most condensed and complete sociological section to be seen anywhere in the world'. Here, a decade before the masques, Geddes was already considering the possibilities of historical drama: responding to paintings of the succession of Scottish kings imagined as a procession, Geddes argues 'Nor can any historic lesson be [...] more vivid, more intense, more picturesque, and more constructive than the actual embodiment of such a procession in actual pageant'. For Geddes, the spectacle of the city, with its stratified accumulations from history, was itself a kind of theatre: 'a city is more than a place in space, it is a drama in time'. The staging of the masques gives this thought its most natural expression.

The medievalism of Geddes' masques reflects an idiosyncratic sense of medieval drama. As Geddes' collaborator Victor Branford defines it, 'The Miracle Play itself epitomized what was known of the origin, history and destiny of man'. Geddes positions the masques as the miracle play's secular counterpart: 'an attempt to shadow forth the long Mystery-Play of the Ascent of Man'. The Masques of learning seek to trace the story of education from prehistory to the present; Scotland and Celtic history are given a prominence surprising in the context of a history of humanity, yet in line with the site of the masques' production and inspiration. Alongside tableaux of Egypt and China are scenes of Hebrew and Indian learning, and the collaborative genesis of the masques is marked in Geddes' acknowledgement of the part played by Edinburgh's substantial body of international students from India in shaping the version of history presented here. Geddes contemplates the possibility of a future Masque of Indian Learning on the strength of this. Later scenes reflect the limitations of the masques' perspective: the Abbasid caliph Harun al-Rashid is incorporated as having 'most fully impressed the European imagination', though Geddes claims that 'we owe the conception as well as the execution of this scene' to Muslim students.

Women are a striking absence within the masques. Geddes' choice of epigraph is telling: 'Let us now praise famous men'. While women were involved as players, their roles are limited. A brief prologue imagines an encounter between a schoolboy and male professor, who examines the books crammed into the boy's bag as a chorus that 'renews the voices of the patriarchal world'. The professor tells the boy that the book 'is not merely a fossil' but 'a spell by which you may recall the past', advising him to exercise body and mind, throwing his ball and eating 'the apple of knowledge'. In doing so, the boy matriculates as student, opening the pageant. Listening to the professor, 'A woman student swiftly takes notes', and Geddes presents her writing as the source of the masque that follows. The woman student is a tantalising presence, but her role is that of a vessel: silent and instrumental. Only a few women appear as historical figures within the masque: Sappho has a fleeting cameo 'with her maidens' (Geddes speaks tersely of 'old and long-enduring aspersions' on her character). Mary, Queen of Scots has a brief vignette imagining her meeting with John Knox to agree the funding of Parish schools, and is celebrated as 'one of the great ladies of the Renaissance'. Elizabeth, however, is absent: 'we may be pardoned for a presentation of the great Elizabethans without Elizabeth; the more since every Pageant of recent years has done her ample justice'.

The effect of the whole is a model of history in which women appear almost exclusively in supporting roles, their greatest contribution as teachers to great men. The rationale for historical drama as a way to engage the emotions is used to present teaching as a woman's role: because education depends 'upon the early arousal and guidance of the emotional life [...] For great teachers who have really achieved vital uplifts in Scottish history we think of Robert Burns' old nurse, and Robert Louis', of Walter Scott's kindly aunts'. Formalised schooling is 'a measure of expediency, during times of decadence of woman'. Geddes even blames women's 'abandonment of the mother's supreme educational guidance', in favour of sensual indulgence, for the fall of the Roman empire.

If the masques' particular content is difficult to reconcile with modern values, their purpose as an engagement with history that complements Geddes' project of urban regeneration is nevertheless inspiring. Geddes' masques anticipate the possibility that in recalling the past, the public might also renew it and shape the future, in the creation of the community brought together by the act of performance, a productive fusion of town and gown (like that made possible in new buildings such as University Hall). The masques evoke the idea that the scenes from history they present might themselves change the fabric of the city too, in the erection of new monuments or the reconstruction of buildings lost to time. History, here, 'is no mere retrospect of the past, nor excavation in it: what it reveals to us, above all, is the past still working on within our apparent present'. The masque is, for Geddes, not only a mystery but also a morality play, a reminder that 'each great step in the progress of culture arises with the growth of the City'.

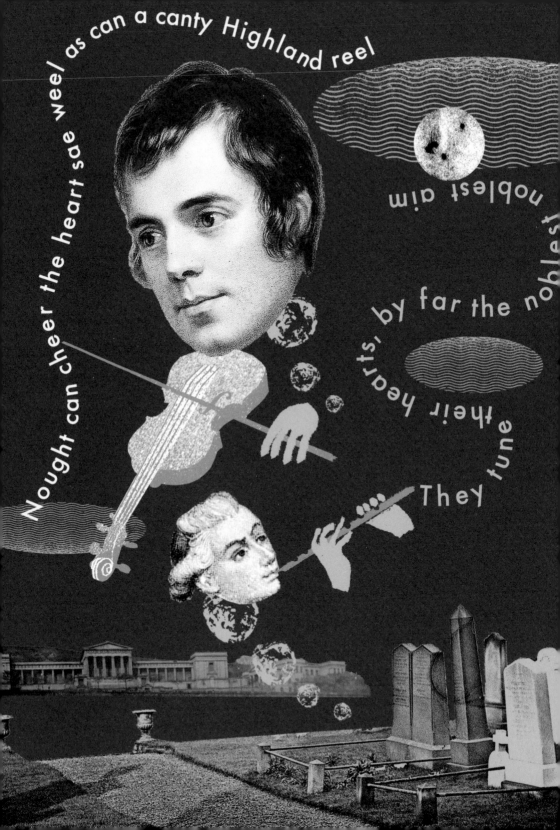

Nought can cheer the heart sae weel as can a canty Highland reel

noblest aim

by far the noblest

their hearts,

They tune

People of the same trade seldom meet together but the conversation ends in a

CONSPIRACY AGAINST THE PUBLIC

OLD TOWN LIMERICKS BY AN EVERGREEN MADAM

PETRA REID

31

Dear, dear old L.S. (see Evergreen 2nd)
mistress of sex that's less than fecund;
in Camera Obscura
(who can obscure her?)
oor hoor tours Master Geddes' Land.

*

There was a piper, a Scottish piper*
piped for a penguin (Emperor),
what's up his kilt's no Riddle:
frostbite from a piddle
and chronic distemper.

*

Consider our man (Sir!) Geddes
discoursing on more and more being less he's
sounding a wee bit like Aristotle
(living by leaves takes some bottle,
you can't be a cynic, like Diogenes).

*

He had a wife called Annie
au fait with Hindustani;
she purchased him a sordid slum
got him to do what Octavia done
(bluestocking karma's canny).

*

O for some red ashlar and white exterior
once pre-owned by Ramsay Senior;
somewhere to hang your dead hair hats
sub New Town aristocrats;
whilst warming a well-licked posterior.

*

That White Horse Inn is not at all cheap now
their platter of Fruits de Mer costs more than half a cow;
phylum mollusca shuckled out the back,
unisexual but with a crack
and messing with your bowels now.

*

Urban planners – future proof Auld Edina!
Facilitate the World to dine on her!
Liz/Bess – Holyrood can host the portaloos!
(Do cyborgs do electric poos?)
No cock or bull in this Regina!

*

Lady Stair's man died of an apoplexion
post a long debate on The Union
pre-Doc Johnson's dictionary
re RP's superiority.
(Jim MacPherson had their bairn – Ossian.)

*

Just behind Ye Olde Christmas Shoppe
a burghal garden suggests local autonomy.
Bring it on! A liberation
of The Celtic imagination,
(might) end this Santa Claus economy!

*

Consider a Mound built of oyster shell
(that's what the excavations tell)
where students live to study wanking
(less kindly known as banking)
– doesn't Nature recycle us well?

*

Parler-moi d'amour et bacterium
in consensual evolution,
free all flotillaries
from concrete pillories –
vanguard for our romantic's revolution!

*

Lucky's Last Word:

James' Court was fair slumious,
Annie G said f***! That's our work cut out for us!
(Wish I had a wife,
less trouble and strife,
more vivendo dicimus.)

*

*Among the adventures triggered by Patrick Geddes' approach to education –
and accommodation – was the Scottish National Antarctic Expedition of 1902–4.
It was during the Scottish National Antarctic Expedition that this classic
photograph, known as 'The Piper and the Penguin', was taken. It shows the
expedition's piper, Gilbert Kerr, braving the elements in a kilt while serenading
an apparently unimpressed emperor penguin.

HIDDEN GEM - 85054

visitors so far this year

HOTELS NOT HOMES

I'm a bin
Drop your
litter in
BY ORDER OF CITY PLANNING

POEMS

ALTERNATE
DEVELOPMENTS

FROM   THE
EVOLUTION OF SEX
BY PATRICK GEDDES
AND J.ARTHUR THOMSON

ALICE
TARBUCK

39

VI. EARLY NUTRITION.—

The early nutrition of the embryo,
yelk material, which is probably richest in the eggs of birds.
The tadpole   exerts itself
at the expense of this inheritance of yelk.
di\ ision of amphibians,
pro\ ided for by
the larva literally living upon itself.

The same is true in elaborate metamorphosis

In the whelk and related forms, a curious cannibalism:
the stronger and older devour.
But in birds
no drop of blood ever passes from mother to offspring,
a very intimate osmotic transfusion.

Lactation: caused by the offspring's demands,
involving cellular disruption and death.
We can understand more readily
'witches' milk'
at birth, puberty, and under pathological conditions,
while cases have been put on record of men who
undergo degeneration, disruption, and expulsion,
put through a course of 'gastric education',
by feeding upon the readily assimilated.

II. ILLUSTRATIONS FROM DARWIN.—

Among invertebrates, jointed-footed animals or arthropods
among crustaceans and spiders,
beautiful illustrations abound.
Spiders often differ from their fiercely coy mates, in smaller size, darker colours
in the power of producing rasping sounds,
the noisy love-calling.
Cicadas 'live happy, having voiceless wives.'
the gemmeous dragonet is flushed with gorgeous colour,
the sea-scorpion {Cottiis scorpius), or the stickleback {Gasterosteus),
transformed,
putting on a wedding-garment.
Every one knows love, its noisy prayer replaced
by the silent appeal of fragrant incense,
the subtler charms of music
that the wooers mainly trust:
the power of charming decides the problem of courtship.

X. NEMESIS OF REPRODUCTION.—

Reproduction in its origin is linked to death.
Organisms, one hears, have to die ; they must therefore reproduce.
A lowly and somewhat enigmatical mature female
terminates her individual life by bursting.
The death is an altogether inevitable consequence in fact, one of the keynotes
—the young live at the expense of the mother, until she is reduced to a mere husk.
The exhaustion is fatal,
and the males are also involved
—an ideal but too unpractical lover
would seem usually to fail and expire prematurely:
death may tragically persist,
as the direct nemesis of love.

MAKE THE CITY AFTER YOUR HEART'S DESIRE

POSITIVE CONTAGION: WHAT UNIVERSITIES ARE FOR

LESLEY McARA

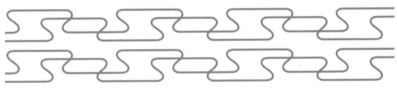

This school strives to adapt itself to meet the wants and needs, the ideas and ideals, of the place and persons concerned. It seeks to undo as little as possible, while planning to increase, the well-being of the people at all levels, from the humblest to the highest.—Patrick Geddes[1]

Patrick Geddes believed that there should be a symbiotic relationship between institutions and their environment, and that education had the capacity to drive social change and active citizenship.[2] Some 100 years after Geddes exegesis, the terrain of contemporary scholarship presents Universities with a number of challenges, not least those arising out of the fast-moving developments in data analytics, digital infrastructure and the applications of machine learning and artificial intelligence. Some commentators have characterised these developments as marking a fourth industrial revolution;[3] others, such as Ian Goldin,[4] as a second renaissance.[5] But whichever label is applied, it is clear that these developments are transforming the ways in which we encounter and understand social phenomena, with profound implications for the ways in which knowledge is produced, purveyed, and consumed, as well as for the ways in which institutions think, act and are held to account. Some commentators have laid emphasis on the far-reaching social, economic and cultural benefits that these advances might procure. Whilst others have highlighted their dystopic possibilities – structurally redundant populations (whole generations innovated out of work), mass surveillance and loss of privacy, unregulated tech conglomerates and manipulated electoral processes.

For me these developments signal the need for a renaissance in the concept of the 'Civic University': a university which places its research and education in the service of the community and one which in Geddes' terms seeks to increase the well-being of people at all levels. Indeed, if we are to realise the promise of data driven innovation for society and mitigate against its darker potential, this will require more effective collaboration and *critical* friendship between Universities, governments, industry and the communities within which they are situated and whom they serve. A truly civic university, however, is one characterised by practical action and not simply platitudes: giving effect to its values through its deeds, and not through words alone.

THE UNIVERSITY AND CIVIC ENGAGEMENT

The University of Edinburgh was founded in 1583 as the *Tounis College* by the Edinburgh Town Council and the values it has embraced, arguably, have reflected, and in turn helped to shape, civic culture within the City itself and Scotland more generally.

The Law Faculty at the University, for example, was established in 1707 and came to full flourishing during the Scottish Enlightenment.[6] Its first Professor held the Regius Chair of Public Law and the Law of Nature and Nations. The very title of this Chair bespoke a particular ethos – encompassing public law which explored the relationship between citizens and the State, natural law which focused on ethics and the rights and duties of persons, and the law of nations which sought to regulate the ways in which jurisdictions across the world interacted.

In the 19th century, the University embraced the concept of the 'democratic intellect',[7] a more generalist approach to education which, it was claimed, distinguished Scottish institutions from their counterparts south of the border in England. Predicated on egalitarian principles, the aim was to open up education to all those who had the academic potential regardless of social station. The approach also had implications for the ways in which the University conducted itself as a community of staff and students and for the purpose of scholarship and its wider impact on society.

The 20th century saw the emergence within Edinburgh of the settlement movement.[8] Its aims were to link town and gown more closely, seeking to alleviate poverty, provide services for those who were disadvantaged and empower communities. A characteristic feature was that students and academics would be resident in settlement houses within disadvantaged communities. An edition of the *The Student* in 1939 (edited at that time by Charles P. McAra) speaks warmly of the many social clubs in the Pleasance that were run by students for the local community, and the pride which the University took in its settlement work.

THE CHALLENGES FACING 21ST CENTURY SCHOLARSHIP

Fast forward 80 years, and universities are now at a new set of crossroads. The purity of sentiment and philosophic framing that characterised earlier eras is under threat from a range of sources both external and internal to higher education. And the mutually constitutive relationship between the University and its wider civic context is in danger of dislocation.

In part this is to do with the extremely complex challenges or 'wicked problems' which society faces. Wicked problems sit across and between government departments, there are no stopping points at which the problem is solved, and solutions often become another problem. Efforts to address wicked problems require a certain form of leadership, one which asks the right questions rather than always seeking to provide the right answers. They require multidisciplinary rather than specialist mindsets, and clumsy rather than elegant theoretical and methodological responses. According to Grint,[9] academics need to adopt the worldview of the *bricoleur* or the *do it yourself craft worker* and understand that no one person has the solution in isolation. Importantly, clumsy approaches involve disruption and challenge but crucially they also require slow scholarship (taking time to build relationships, and time to unravel and interrogate complexity). Against this backdrop, the revolution in data, digital and artificial intelligence presents an intriguing paradox: as both part of the problem and part of potential solutions. For example, multiple deprivation can be characterised as a wicked problem: certain communities across Edinburgh over many decades have experienced poorer health, lower life expectancy, lower levels of educational attainment, and higher levels of unemployment, than their more affluent neighbours. The revolution in artificial intelligence may exacerbate unemployment in these areas, and yet the revolution in big data analytics and digital may drive innovative solutions in terms of public policy reform.

As readers will be aware, however, expert knowledge has been increasingly denigrated by politicians and some elements of the news media, and thus our capacity to offer the form of leadership needed to tackle wicked problems is somewhat fragile. Notorious examples are MP Michael Gove's exhortation, during the Brexit campaign, that 'people in this country have had enough of experts',[10] and President Donald Trump's tweets challenging scientists on a range of issues from Ebola to climate change.[11] The multiplicity of information, fed via the internet, and the capacity for emotive and populist responses to be catapulted into the public imagination through social media, has created a context in which expert synthesis and commentary is needed more than ever but is often disregarded, treated with condescension or reacted to with hate-speech.

Adding to these difficulties, the academic role too is changing in response to what some argue is an increased commodification of education. At its extremes, the view of the student as consumer drives an instrumental, specialist, approach to graduate production and in the process puts at risk the modes of learning which are most likely to result in the biggest leaps in knowledge (for example stretching the critical capacity of students to work across academic disciplines and infusing risk-taking into pedagogy as a positive attribute). Contemporary modes of assessing research and teaching performance (via the Research Excellence Framework and the Teaching Excellence Framework) are creating path-dependencies in terms of the types of research output and teaching practice that become highly rated; generating an ever-more fast-paced and reactive culture.

Closer to home, the evolution of Edinburgh as a globalised city also presents challenges as much as opportunity. The major influx of tourism, for example, is concentrating in key areas, putting local services and infrastructure under pressure and displacing residents.[12] The University is perceived by some as a contributing factor, deriving, in part, from its evolving architectural imprint. Care needs to be taken that as a University we work with communities to tackle, and not exacerbate, the complex and wicked challenges which globalisation brings. And one of the ways in which the University of Edinburgh is aiming to meet such challenges is through the creation of the Edinburgh Futures Institute (EFI).

THE CIVIC RESPONSIBILITIES OF THE EDINBURGH FUTURES INSTITUTE

The high-level vision of the Edinburgh Futures Institute is to support humanity's navigation of complex futures[13] and the activities which will shape its first 15 years of operation are linked to the data driven innovation programme of the Edinburgh City and South East Scotland City Region Deal.[13] In attempting to ensure that society reaps the full benefits of data driven innovation, EFI is consciously drawing on the historical values of the University outlined above in terms of enlightenment, democracy, empowerment and mobilisation. The Institute has four distinctive features.

Firstly, EFI embraces a challenge-based and applied approach, recognising that the response to many of the wicked problems facing society lies in radical ways of working across disciplines, which bring together, and at-scale, the arts, humanities and social sciences with the natural sciences, medicine and data science. In progressing this approach, we are also mindful of the myriad ethical challenges that data driven innovation may bring, and a core dimension of our work will be to explore and solve such challenges, working to build public trust and confidence and to ensure that institutions which harvest and manipulate huge swathes of personal data can be held to account.

Secondly, all EFI research and education will be co-produced in partnership with government, industry and the wider public, including local communities. Here the aim is to build a genuinely democratic approach to knowledge production, recognising that academics do not always know the right questions to ask and that collaboration is needed to design and implement innovation.

Thirdly, EFI is developing a life-long educational offer that is open to all who have the potential to study regardless of capacity to pay. Our participatory ethos will embrace undergraduate, postgraduate, continuing professional development, and executive education as well as access programmes and open learning.

Fourthly, EFI is to be located in the former Royal Infirmary of Edinburgh on Lauriston Place: and our aim is to create a symbiotic relationship between the intellectual and outreach programmes of EFI and the built environment. The old hospital was designed according to Florence Nightingale's precepts: to avoid contagion. We want to disrupt these precepts to create a place where cross-infection between disciplines is encouraged, where students and the wider public will encounter industry and government partners. Above all we are committed to bringing new life to a much loved civic building, giving it significant social purpose for the next hundred years or more.

Our agenda is ambitious and none of this is going to be easy. Importantly, we recognise that success depends on the support and collaboration of community partners. The old motto above the main entrance to our building is 'patet omnibus', which means open to all: an ethos for EFI that is literally set in stone!

In conclusion, I want to return to Patrick Geddes and his exhortation that institutions should aim to increase the well-being of people at all levels, from the humblest to the highest. In aspiring to be civic-minded the University will be judged by the ways in which it conducts itself and by the broader impact of its research and education. The wider contexts in which we operate create a myriad of challenges, the resolution to which have a fundamental role to play in sustaining planetary health and well-being and in maintaining a society underscored by civility, justice and rights. Can the University rise to these challenges and work in partnership with others? We can, we must, we will!

1. Geddes, Patrick (1947) Town Planning in Kapurthala. A Report to H.H. the Maharaja of Kapurthala, 1917 In Jacqueline Tyrwhitt (ed.). *Patrick Geddes in India*. London: Lund Humphries. p. 24

2. https://www.nls.uk/learning-zone/politics-and-society/patrick-geddes

3. Schwab, K. (2016) *The Fourth Industrial Revolution*, World Economic Forum

4. https://www.rse.org.uk/wp-content/uploads/2019/02/Our-Age-of-Discovery.pdf

5. https://www.rse.org.uk/wp-content/uploads/2019/02/Our-Age-of-Discovery.pdf

6. https://www.law.ed.ac.uk/sites/default/files/2019-05/Learning%20and%20the%20Law%201st%20 Edition-%20Digital%20version.pdf

7. Davie, George Elder (2000) *The Democratic Intellect: Scotland and her Universities in the Nineteenth Century.* Edinburgh: Edinburgh University Press

8. http://www.socialwork.ed.ac.uk/centenary/timeline/events/edinburgh_university_settlement_begins

9. Grint, K. (2008), Wicked Problems and Clumsy Solutions: the Role of Leadership, *Clinical Leader,* Vol. I Number II, December

10. https://www.ft.com/content/3be49734-29cb-11e6-83e4-abc22d5d108c

11. https://institutions.newscientist.com/article/2099977-what-donald-trump-has-said-about-science-and-why-hes-wrong/

12. https://www.scotsman.com/news/politics/citizen-group-launches-easter-rising-to-defend-edinburgh-from-over-tourism-and-developers-1-4912029

13. https://efi.ed.ac.uk/

14. https://ddi.ac.uk/

Pilgrims climb the cobbled street

SOME SORE AT HEART
AND DRAGGING FEET,
FIND PEACE

EDINBURGH CASTLE
MEMORIAL PEACE
GARDEN

INSTEAD, INTO THE GARDEN I GO

JANET DICK

I grew up with farm boys. They had money and cars. I learned something of the class system from them but never learned how to drive a car. A lifetime of rage against inequality has done me nothing but good and one less car driver has saved the world from another nutter behind the wheel.

My love of the countryside has remained with me though, during forty years of living in the middle of central Edinburgh. My home is in the Grassmarket, it came with the man I'd set my heart on. We have north and south facing windows and on every one there is a window box filled all year round with colour. The south facing ones have large climbing jasmine with sweet scented blooms early and late in the year, and pyracantha stretches out and upwards, offering branches to eager perching birds. Bird feeders attract goldfinches, greenfinches, chaffinches, bullfinches, blue tits, coal tits, great tits, dunnocks, robins, wrens and blackbirds.

But we are selective: I chase off starlings, along with feral pigeons and grey squirrels – they don't need my expensive seeds and they keep the smaller birds away. Policing the greedy beggars can be a full-time activity. Shouting 'fuck off' and waving dishtowels works. However, nothing will deter a sparrowhawk from picking off fledglings as they enjoy their free meal. I've observed mostly male sparrowhawks but once a female took young birds from the feeders too. We've also had a visit from a juvenile peregrine who sat among the pigeons. He was tolerated for a time, before being chased from his perch by one of the braver pigeons.

Gardening in a flat in the middle of a city is a life-affirming activity, and not just for me. Neighbours and passers-by look up and notice. Until recently I also had two planters out on the street, by the front door. Large prickly pyracantha grew there safely for four years until some drunken eejits smashed them and rubbished the flowering primula. In the summer, sweet peas grew up and around the prickly branches and whenever I watered them passers-by would tell me how beautiful they were and how much they liked seeing them. I now have new metal planters to replace the broken ones. I'm not for giving up.

But poking about in planters and window baskets has its limits if you were raised in the countryside and the land is where you want to be. Five years ago the council relented, after a lot of pleading from residents, and allowed us the use of a neglected greenspace, of historic importance, at the foot of West Port. Since then I have been an active outdoor gardener and it has been like a second home to me.

West Port Garden is owned by the City of Edinburgh Council, an original 'Patrick Geddes garden' dating from 1910, one of around 70 gardens established on derelict sites across the Old Town. Designed by Geddes's daughter Norah, and run by women volunteers, it provided tenement children of the area access to outdoor space to play and enjoy nature. The Grassmarket has very few families with young children now; life here is not for the fainthearted. What is politely referred to as the Night Time Economy wreaks havoc on people's lives.

The garden is not tucked away and yet countless people remark on how often they have passed it without noticing that a garden is there. It's not what you expect to find in the middle of the drinking mecca. Fenced in and with a locked gate, the garden is protected from the scale of damage that would befall it from a constant stream of visitors. But it opens its gates to all every Sunday and more regularly throughout the week during summer months. I am one of about twelve gardeners who weed, dig, plant and nurture this precious space. My own commitment to the garden is singularly selfish: without it I'd have to pack up and go back to Perthshire.

Being able to spend time outdoors, often completely alone, amid the sight and sounds of nature, has given me an essential coping method for living in the city. But I also Love My Neighbour. Without any religious dogma to complicate this love, I care about the people around me. Gardening fits beautifully into my angry crusade to make the world a better place; it's impossible to garden without thinking of the wider world. The choices you make when you weed, dig, plant and nurture will carry evidence for a long time. You learn not to harm living things. Slugs, bugs, weeds and cat shit all have a place and there are plenty of creative solutions for how to get rid of the blighters without killing them all.

My principal intention at the start of my outdoor gardening was to create a place of beauty for everybody to enjoy. Growing vegetables was categorically NOT on my list. My Perthshire parents have a large garden where more courgettes than you could eat in one lifetime are produced, along with potatoes, cabbages, beetroots, onions, garlic, leeks, peas, beans and duck eggs. I don't want all those responsibilities. But it's impossible to have the use of land and not consider growing your own food. Indeed, I'd go as far as to say that it's immoral *not* to grow your own food if you have the opportunity. Land use and misuse have become a major conversation topic for the gardeners of West Port. We've become politically aware of the issues surrounding how our food is produced, what's in it, what it's doing to us and more significantly what it's doing to the planet. The West Port Garden has excellent quality soil; after 40 years of being left alone nature has worked her magic and produced rich, dark, productive matter. But our careful planting for biodiversity will carry this legacy only so far. The toxic effects from traffic may mean that home grown potatoes become as popular for dinner as hemlock...

This little garden of ours has its part to play in wider efforts to look after the natural world. Repeatedly we hear and share the same stories with visitors on open days: land is precious and we need to take better care of it. Our garden is also an essential corridor in Edinburgh for a fragile population of living things, birds, bees, butterflies, connecting them all to larger greenspaces which are equally under threat. Trees, hedges and grassland are all at risk from a variety of sources. The farming community is only one of many seeking to claim land for increased production at a cost to wildlife and the environment.

Our own city has shown a blind indifference to some of the best wildlife legislation in the world. Contractors and developers prune and fell trees in the nesting season; they remove healthy green growth in public spaces to 'keep out rough sleepers'; they strim whole areas of garden stock to make it look 'tidy'; they hire out gardens and greenspaces for events that cause long term damage to the soil; they hang artificial lighting in trees to the detriment of birds and insects. Add to that the damage done by the planning and licensing departments, who lack any interest in biodiversity and a healthy environment.

About nine years ago a bucket load of European money was spent on 'environmental improvements' for the Grassmarket (it even won awards). Perhaps the word 'environment' lost something in the translation. The *natural* environment was ruined. They removed large, much-loved poplar trees and replaced them with container-grown oaks and limes. None of these trees will ever grow to the size of the original ones, and that affects the bird population. Few if any will ever nest in these new trees. The large poplars also gave room for rooks to roost. We've pretty much lost them and within months of the new trees being planted there was a sizeable increase in pigeon and gull numbers, scavengers who plague our sleep with their night time plundering of bins, discarded takeaways and vomit.

Small changes make a big difference. I campaigned for planters to be brought into the area to brighten up the look of the place. Again I saw the impact that a little bit of nature has on everything around it. Wrens peck around the ivy then take off to land on my own planters in search of a grub or two. Blackbirds do the same. But food alone is not enough to sustain living things. They need water too. At my own window box I'm happy to live with filthy windows from the splashings of blackbirds bathing and sipping at a dish of water. One of the gardeners at West Port filled a large metal dish with stones and water and within minutes of setting it up the first blackbird arrived. Regularly we are delighted now by the bathing blackbirds.

Part of my life is like a scene from *Little House on The Prairie* – I have surrounded myself with the beauty of nature. I am happy. Cut from that to a recurring scene from Fellini's *Satyricon*. Not happy. Edinburgh has more licensed premises than any other city in the whole of Scotland. We have a monoculture in Grassmarket; there are so many pubs very little else can thrive. The night-time economy has impacted heavily on the day-time businesses and their response to this has been to turn the area into an Events Space! For nearly eight years locals had to endure not only disturbance during their sleeping hours but during their wakening ones too. Amplified bands and street entertainment rocked up every weekend along with markets, marathons and anything that justified a crowd for an afternoon. The Greater Grassmarket Business Improvement District (BID) exploited every square foot of 'common land' with the support of Scottish Government and City of Edinburgh Council solely for the benefit of businesses. They created nothing but a lot of noise and upset and after five years they left seeking pastures new; a bigger, badder BID is now planned for the WHOLE Old Town!

My life has been shaped by decision-makers who have no vision and who are replaced every four years by myopic clones. I have wasted so much time listening to these people. I have used every tool available to me through the democratic process. I've written to and met with councillors, MPs, MSPs and senior members of staff, I've joined committees and set up residents groups, I've wrangled at Licensing and Planning committees, I've done TV and radio slots, I've hung banners from my windows and I've marched the length and breadth of the country in protests. To date it's done little or nothing for me or for the city. We get tokenistic changes that placate people for a short time but very little has ever been achieved with lasting effect. Things get worse.

Outside my front door we have two glass phials measuring levels of nitrogen dioxide. They show that throughout the year my family is breathing gigantic levels of toxicity. Cars, vans, lorries, delivery vehicles to all the pubs, cafes, restaurants and hotels, along with all the fucking tourist buses clog up the roads and our bronchial tubes. The planners approved this despite a shitload of regulations which set limits and better standards. Whose interests they are serving is a question you'd have to ask them because I'm done with useless talk.

Instead, into the garden I go. Throughout the year and in all weather. I have a wardrobe now of permanently grubby clothes. I still enjoy choosing which dirty frock will go well with the dirty leggings and be topped off by practical colourful woollen socks and a pair of shorn-off wellies. For the company I keep I am perfectly attired and if the socks are bright enough I sometimes manage to upstage the goldfinches. But woman cannot live by birds alone; humankind forces itself upon us all, whether we invite it or not.

A happy band of gardeners are we, working collectively at times and, best of all, silently alone. Any group of people will have their differences (and we do) but on one single issue we are all agreed: no weed killer and no pesticides. It works so long as everybody is happy to do their bit, for this rule can result in repetitive and back-breaking work. Some recently acquired prayer mats have helped protect our knees and who knows, perhaps our industry will channel some divine force into glorious new garden growth. Good as the mats are though, they do not protect us from the hardest pain of all: The Committee!

A residents' association watches the work of the gardeners. It makes no contribution to the daily toil and holds the strings to funds. We manage (just) by raising money from public donations, which irks The Committee. A great amount of energy is spent considering ways to work with it or around it and goes nowhere. We spend our money on plants, tools and repair work, it's hard to understand why anybody would be put out by this. My own journey into gardening was in response to years of wasted time at meetings, being part of committees and organisations that enjoyed talking and doing very little. I can't be part of that process any more. My body tells me with every aching muscle and joint that ACTION is what counts. Hoeing and sowing, not hoping and moping.

It brings rewards. The garden is gratefully admired by hundreds of locals and visitors. For the gardeners this praise is encouraging: our work is recognised and acknowledged by others. A long list of trees, shrubs, flowers, bulbs and other organic matter could be provided as further evidence here; but it would not do justice to the garden and the gardeners. You have to see it for yourself. Maybe even get dirty...

It's impossible to spend time outdoors amongst trees, plants, birds and other quietly busy, buzzing things, without being in awe. Every time I walk into our garden I stand still to watch and listen. Leaving the noise of the traffic behind me I look forward and upwards to the bird feeders amongst the boughs of an elm. The garden continues with its own routine and if I am patient, I can enjoy ten minutes of feeding, preening, bathing, in-flight squabbling (goldfinches excel in this), and the bird song of up to six different varieties. Robins, dunnock and blue tits will remain at their activities if I walk slowly and further into their territory. Nothing quite equals the joy of being allowed to get close to such small, vulnerable and trusting life. The goldfinches, greenfinches and bullfinches will give you a two-minute soap opera if you stand stock still. Their hasty retreat is no less enjoyable. A marvellous flurry of reds, yellows, greens, and blacks with high pitched tones warning others that an intruder is amongst them. The garden belongs to them really.

the city we

DREAM

we finally inhabit

MIND HOW

HELENA FORNELLS

LILA MATSUMOTO

MOONSUN

Lunar   landscape   someone
tried to cut rocks in precise
shapes here   squares long
vertical and horizontal lines.

You have to look at this twice
think where did they take all
the rocks from where now void
is delimited by machine cuts.

Lunar landscape water near
us and its sounds the colour
changes from the wild to the
linear pools where they had

tried to build   and failed
dreams of wellness
& wealth which we could not
bear to look at.

Let's close our eyes –
we walk on and discover new
deluded   projects   unfinished
palaces all around:

The Economy masked as Art
we discuss over dinner lunar
rocks surrounding

rocks we had walked on
during the day.

That economic failure but the
sun the sea and its
salt like ice on bitten rock

are a pleasure.

Helena Fornells

APO– PHANAI

I had found the word 'yes' ... which denotes acquiescence,
self-abandon, relaxation, the end of all resistance.
  James Joyce, Letter to Harriet Shaw Weaver

Molly, for you, I am
going to calibrate the word:

Affirmative meaning eclipsing –
listen, we can't know God

in the way we know our mother.
With the *word*,

reason drifts like a duck downriver
so we hope for silence,

deny all else – do, for now,
something other than

speaking. Hear the denial of my
intention to speak of you today –

I tell everyone they will not see
you

          confined in yellowing
letters. I am confined

by speaking through an infatuation
with negation – but when we,

silent, say no and begin to trace
the outlines of the feared omission,

we will be raised, like
flowers emerging in shadow-space,
by virtue of this living absence.

Helena Fornells

AUBADE

The city is a body ringing itself with sound.
Two voices, three, in clarion getting louder
carrying down the street.

Remind yourself of death each time an elevator
opens, as the song that implores in four-four
the watch to be turned face down.

Pain is always circumscribed in music's sweetness
calling origin and disappearance of sound. Is the city
then not a stance against the contingency

of ends, dorming everything before the raid?
Tarrying in the opus: food everywhere spilling
out, gleaming globes of fruit, white-silver

starlights garlanding the street. Also: a churn
to cream wealth, the highest botching of an earlier
wood, of flesh seared insensate. Do you live

the things or observe them? What voice effusive
and quick, thin and coercing? From door
or window to the sleeping city – what must you sing?

Lila Matsumoto

Z U S !

M O N I C A
D A T T A

Zoe had been petitioning to go to the shore ever since they arrived. In a marshy patch she pushed the clay upwards so that it yielded to the ocean. Bliss was not for her: instead she was subject to an infantile tubular metaphysics. Inside the building, mumpsy kogelvissen and the enormous schildpadden – everyone's favourite grandgrandgrandgrandparents – wept in vitrines, with new toy names. She looked for eggs and wondered if she could cultivate a better exposition.

Ursula, four years younger, six inches shorter, somewhat less blond than Zoe, preferred sand and mashed her toes into the cold ground till she squealed. The seashore was unbearable without text. In the aquarium she gazed at the fine print on the biologist's scuba tank as he humiliated the largest of the schildpadden.

Sigrid, four years younger, six inches shorter, somewhat less blond than Ursula, slipped at the shoreline and soaked to the skin. She had broken into het huis van de pinguïns and no one knew she was missing till they returned. All the sisters agreed the aquascaping was naïve.

Zoe subsisted on tea from home with sinaasappelstukjes and the occasional woody apple plucked from a tree lining the fat streets, nourished by the meagre river. She slipped her dinner under the table to Sigrid, who scraped the plate into an empty koektrommel. It rained all day.

Ursula agreed that the river was meagre. Better was the bay, primordial with tea and thick, sulphuric crude oil. (Everyone loved tea and crude oil.) It rained all night.

Sigrid, satisfied after both dinners, would set her alarm clock, a phosphorescent Voronoi giraffe called Esmildred, to midnight so they could read after everyone had gone to sleep. Esmildred stretched her luminous neck at a picture of a girl rowing a boat through Birmingham, where the canals were filled with milky breakfast tea. 'Oh, Esmildred, I also love water!' Sigrid whispered.

Zoe, who often boasted that English was her worst subject, was learning to endure lengthy periods without saying anything. On day three she said ik verveel me. Now all the burgers in school wanted to be her friend. She spent a weekend in New York photographing her Sharpie marker-bruised toes holding up small syringes of Valentina hot sauce. When everyone on the internet liked it, she chucked her mobile in the harbour.

Ursula, reflecting on the profligate disuse of canals in the United States, suggested that the rank character of their surroundings emerged from a mutation; the burgers had repressed their seafaring history and had a chemical swamp instead of a collective unconscious. There was only one thing left to do: in unison she and Zoe cheered, 'Let us effect a canalisation scheme throughout the United States of America!'

Sigrid was so excited, even though no one would tell her what a canalisation scheme was! At school the next day she coated her street crossing workbook in blue watercolour and had to stand in the corner all day, its own reward.

Zoe, in a van Doesburg monograph, found a series of gouache sketches to inform the first few iterations: they would square off the eighteen-thousand-two-hundred-forty-one canals in the United States – all wrecks – if one included Alaska and Hawaii, which, thanks to the ocean, would cause no problems of continuity.

Ursula agreed that all the canals should be orthogonal, bloated to accommodate the movement of boats. They would supersede the existing highway system and reintroduce the burgers to water.

Sigrid squeezed oil paints into ice cube trays and chanted, 'Jef-fer-son! Jef-fer-son! Jef-fer-son!'

Zoe discovered a working canal in New York State just two hundred kilometres away that went not only through Amsterdam, but Rotterdam, London, Frankfurt, Palmyra, Syracuse, Troy and Medina!

Ursula said that two hundred kilometres were nearly the length of the Netherlands; forcing the burgers to cycle such a distance would tire them, increasing their receptivity to current ideas.

Sigrid tumbled towards them on a tiny violet driewieler: the hill was so steep! Zoe and Ursula gracefully backed away, cackling.

Zoe, the next time they went to the shore, led her sisters down the coast to rocky patches, where the boulders were soft and suggested boring the canals with ice. Films with fjords in them hypnotised the subjects so profoundly that they collapsed in despair afterwards.

Ursula moved rocks to form walls. Injections of whimsy – karst formations, icebergs, predatory wildlife; imitation Atlantises constructed by octopuses – would lull the burgers into pleasure.

Sigrid scoffed. Fools fell for false fjords.

Zoe was born on Huidenstraat between Keizersgracht and Herengracht.

Ursula was born on Elandstraat between Lijnbaansgracht and Prinsengracht.

Sigrid was born in hospital further out. This explained everything.

Zoe was the blondest, on the way to blue hair. Bleaching turned it cheap biro red-black, then brittle rust till one day it broke Labrador yellow.

Ursula was less blonde than Zoe. She had alopecia areata and refused the silky temple-scraped bob for which she had been fitted, favouring instead a wardrobe of bright synthetics the texture of fishing line. Nearly every day since they arrived she wore a French ultramarine mullet that turned Zoe green.

Sigrid was less blonde than Ursula because she wasn't blond at all. Airport security the world over spent hours examining her head for explosives. In Heathrow a famous sculptor – after having assured customs he didn't know who headed ISIS in his home country – witnessed this routine procedure and begged to purchase her hair so that he could make the blackest black none more black pigment and anything it touched would disappear!

Zoe's first attempt at a master plan, scolded Ursula, redlining shakily, was, at best, unrefined: how much farmland was she planning to flood? She would have to fix everything.

Ursula then critiqued Zoe's naive earthmoving procedure, her total ignorance of rock formation, the historical precedent of canalisation in the United States – the burgers did not require two whole generations to forget – and the withered husk that was the Colorado River. Zoe crumpled up a page and after it bounced off Ursula's spectacles ordered her to build it.

Sigrid operated the lorry that carried the document: one thousand A0 pages weighed eighty kilogrammes.

Zoe's oma grew up above the rubbishripe North Canal and knew all the ghost stories. Through mad laughter she told them all about headless priests and their beloved black dogs. Crashtrain stray limbs. Boiled potato children. Pregnant girl buried: she knew all about Dutch schooling.

Ursula worried about presenting the scheme before Parlement and was sure it would be vetoed by the minister-president who had spent much of his childhood in Jakarta.

Sigrid didn't say anything. Every time they visited she wanted to go into the water herself, which was more exciting than the stuff back home.

Zoe on the other hand was confident Parlement would approve the canalisation scheme, except for some of the proposed cryptozoological creatures. Het Monster van Loch Ness didn't have a single counselling appointment till next year.

Ursula, via an expensive, Immarsat-facilitated call, put Lagarfljótsormurinn on speaker: worms were socially undesirable and excellent listeners. Routinely discriminated against for their sliminess, sexuality – half hermaphrodite, half male – and ability to survive being cut in half, Lagarfljótsormurinn – despite being a bit psychic – had been continuously heartbroken for all Lagarfljótsormurinn's six hundred seventy-one years. As a baby worm in medieval Iceland Lagarfljótsormurinn was placed in a tiny jewel box on top of a gold ring but one day curled up inside it and started getting fat. When the young girl who kept Lagarfljótsormurinn found out she screamed and threw out the entire box. Ever since, Lagarfljótsormurinn would blind anyone who looked at Lagarfljótsormurinn, and poisoned the fields. Now Lagarfljótsormurinn was condemned to life at the bottom of the lake.

Sigrid began to cry with Lagarfljótsormurinn. Zoe and Ursula were also very sad. The canals had to stand for something. They had to stand for Lagarfljótsormurinn.

Zoe read that if the canals flooded, the world would become a pitch-black egg.

Ursula watched, on her mobile, the underwater explosion of a plastics factory. It was too dangerous to take aerial photographs, but bits of hat were expelled into the air before returning to their swampy birthplace.

Sigrid's mobile rang: it was Het Monster van Loch Ness! They turned on the camera: she floated on a velvet crimson pillow as smaller monster footmen adjusted her legs and belly for comfort. She beamed regally and agreed not only to provide any required counsel but to preside over the ceremony.

Zoe gasped. The American president had been ousted! It seemed the burgers would not, as predicted, coronate a queen like the rest of the civilised world; instead a petrol-soaked basketball had become the new ruler and planned to build a hundred-meter seawall around the perimeter of the country. Now they would have to wait months to present the plan before Parlement.

Ursula didn't blame the burgers for not wanting to welcome in water: she knew water was not their *friend*, per se. It was many things, majestic things, extraordinary things, but not their verdommen *pal*.

Sigrid came running in: Parlement said they would entertain the canalisation scheme!

Zoe, after a long night of travel, was nervous about presenting the scheme to Parlement: what if they didn't understand? What if they, themselves niet normaal, said it was niet normaal to effect an orthogonal canalisation scheme throughout the United States? If she rolled her eyes and shook her head and said niet normaal, would it help or get them be deported? The girls stepped up to the podium.

Ursula, towering over a man who assumed the girls would need step stools, did most of the talking. She fielded questions about not using enough crude oil and assured them it would be there if only for decorative purposes; every year there would be a competition in every canal region to make the best illuminated crude oil balloon sculpture. 'Niet normaal,' hissed Zoe.

Sigrid stood on her toes as the votes were counted. 'Nee.' 'Jee.' 'Nee.' 'Jee.' 'Jee.' 'Nee.' 'Jee.' 'Jee.' 'Nee!' 'Jee!' 'Jee!' 'Jee!' Hoera! They were going to do it! They were going to effect an orthogonal canalisation scheme throughout the United States!

Zoe's new zoning plan, despite the recommendations of Parlement, squared off the existing topography. She decided to name each zone based on animals the burgers had been working to make extinct (Kariboezone; Zeehondenregio) and the entire scheme Olifantgracht, because they needed to soak in the shame.

Ursula said it was redundant to have an elephant in an elephant, and the animals should be ones that the burgers already killed, like the trekduif.

Sigrid said that Zoe could name the scheme after Airavata, the beloved elephant of the god Indra, but only Esmildred would listen.

Zoe's suspicions were confirmed as she met with state and local officials: the burgers were real failures at this canal thing. In the narrowest country they could find, they designed a system of locks so bad they had to install their own police and kill thousands of workers.

Ursula, addressing protesters, tried to assuage their fears: the sisters didn't know enough people to make their own police. Robots would dig the canals. This brought about more rage; they had heard the scheme would provide employment.

Sigrid shouted, 'Everyone's new job is to take care of the elephants!' and with that an 'ahhh' floated about the crowd before the protests resumed.

Zoe asked, 'What is a quart?' They sent for a sample kit of iron weights to help them understand the archaic system of the burgers and had to collect it from an ocean liner. Was a quart a pond? Two ponds? The ton was not so bad, only half a scheepslast, or half a million herring.

Ursula said, 'One-fourth of a gallon or one-two-hundred-fourth of an okshoofd, or three-point-two-two mingles.'

Sigrid said a gallon was five trout. They all nodded.

Zoe had created some canals with radial symmetry that would interlock the main waterways to attract buitenaardsen according to farmers and the architects of Stonehenge who said they preferred round forms.

Ursula felt it would be too much water, turning the landmass to even more of a swamp. Too much digging and wasted soil. Besides, centuries later, ruimtewezens tired of circles and were too smart for bait. What exactly did Zoe expect the aliens to do?

Sigrid drew a pretty sequence of spirals on one of the draft plans. 'Maybe if the circles were together, like this?' Her sisters looked at it and sneered. 'You're wrong, Sigrid.' 'Concentric circles are a waste of time, Sigrid.' 'That's not what a concentric circle is, Zoe!' 'Well there are still too many, Sigrid.' 'Yeah, why can't you spend your time being more productive by moving the weights around, Sigrid?' 'God, Sigrid is such a waste of time.' 'Ruimteverspilling.' 'In cirkels.' 'Tijdverspilling.' 'Vicieuze cirkels.'

Zoe opened the window. There were hundreds of people outside, shouting 'Get out, Petrus Stuyvesant!' 'Except that each of you has two legs!' 'We should not mention that we have noticed the fact of your ethnic minority status but that is one of your only differences which is not to say it makes you any better or worse than he!' 'Go back to Holland with all six of your legs!' 'Cricket!' 'Ladybug!' 'Fire ant!' 'Every ant!' 'Broken spider not that we discriminate against the disabled!' Zoe adored Petrus Stuyvesant, who had saved the burgers from drinking and knifing themselves to death not to mention the English and they still named a cigarette after him.

Ursula had already explained that Petrus Stuyvesant was the most notorious slave owner in Nieuw Amsterdam, a racist and antisemiet who left behind masses of excavated soil from ditches. His ghost was still around. Zoe scoffed, 'That was probably someone else.'

Sigrid, in tears, put Esmildred, a roll of Verkade digestives and a pocket torch in her rugzak and went in the freight elevator.

Zoe, at the press conference, couldn't see a thing in the bright lights. Hundreds of dogsnose microphones all barking. She couldn't understand a word. 'Wijlhaaland gebussmoonee furdekoonaels?' 'Oordekoonaels perdaar mootseekus kantraabooschon foorduwaal?' 'Oofyu beld dokoonaals wattelhaffenwitte trains?' 'Why?'

Ursula did most of the talking. 'No.' 'No.' 'The trains will still be trains because of bridges and aqueducts.' 'We feel that a canalisation scheme, if effected throughout the United States, will provide an efficacious system of transport. It will force burgers to respect the gorgeous mercilessness of water.'

Sigrid listened to the interview from the train as the power lines rushed above her head. She knelt on the seat as they crossed a big canal – which might have been the sea – and gazed at the hippopotamuses.

Zoe sighed after another bewildering presentation to the Cupboard. 'Ursula: it's time for a coup. Some of the weights and measures are substantial enough to help with the task.'

Ursula said that one did not stage a coup against the Cupboard who merely provided advice. If she wanted to stage a coup it was because she had always wanted to stage a coup and maybe she should just do that instead.

Sigrid and Esmildred found a job cooking pannekoeken and said anyone could create round forms with flour and eggs and milk barring modern allergy but did not intend to imply it would be easy to implement an orthogonal canalisation scheme throughout the United States; although roundness could be approximated by angles from a distance, the inverse was not necessarily true.

Zoe occasionally showed up for trigonometry. Teachers understood her priorities were elsewhere. She directed discussions to suit her purposes. 'What about Peixder-type vierkantsvergelijking, where the vectors are orthogonal according to the strictest of axioms as established by Ratz? Does one also need to test for Ulam-Hyers stability?'

Ursula was annoyed by Zoe's tijdverspilling. She wouldn't even ask after the passage of persons, animals and aquatic vehicles, instead embarrassing them all by name-dropping mathematicians she wished to befriend.

Sigrid and Esmildred, although they did not win, placed well in a folk dancing competition. Despite their love of seahorses, the other dancers were afraid of Zoe and were sure it was worth the rule of a child dictator just to effect an orthogonal canalisation scheme throughout the United States. Sigrid said their visas would expire soon and they had to return to school in Holland. Each dancer shed a single tear and squabbled over which of them should host Sigrid and Esmildred.

Zoe, just before dawn, wore the jacket she had been forced to wear in winter even though it was certainly not cold enough to stroll the riverside, chunky with ice. The river bloated crablike into the bay, where penguin mosaics floated on whaleskin. It was difficult to move the boats; burgers at work shouted ja ja ja ja ja ja to one another. Zoe wanted to take out a tile into the sea on a starless night, so cold she would smell of nothing and the sharks would stay away and where there were neither burgers nor canals.

Ursula was gasifying biomass to produce cold, fluffy clouds. Even whilst wearing gloves designed for space exploration from the NSO her hands were frostbitten but she didn't care. She hoped Zoe would never come home.

Sigrid and Esmildred went for a long walk in Texas. They followed the cacti, blooming lush to the river, and waded through the shallow water. The Mexican douaneambtenaars demanded to know what they thought they were doing. Sigrid was, from habit, going to say that she and Esmildred planned to effect an orthogonal canalisation scheme throughout the United States, but didn't want to lie.

Zoe updated the orthogonal canalisation scheme to merge with the canals in Mexico City: it was a *colonialisation* scheme! 'We devised a borderless, rhizomatic system that would hijack the power paradigm and encourage cycling,' she explained to one of the architects.

Ursula said the whole scheme had already been lightly etched into the soil.

Sigrid and Esmildred commandeered a trajinera called Violette to float through the city, looking up at square pink trees and listening to birds then cars then crickets then laughter then cranes then trucks and pneumatic drills then drums then wind. When Violette flipped over and tried to drown them the horizon went to smoke and the trees to fire before the sky fell in.

Zoe saw water rush through the doorjamb. She thought they were going to die but it was the goddess Thalassa, who gave Zoe and Ursula the most beautiful, warm hug, like swimming on the summer solstice. Being filled with water, she saturated the drawing set. Thalassa said, 'I am very proud of you for effecting an orthogonal canalisation scheme throughout the United States, despite some local discomfort. I will take you for ice cream very soon.'

'Esmildred and Sigrid seem to be doing very well,' she added. 'But sometimes one can have too much water.'

Ursula asked, 'Have you seen Sigrid?'

'Sigrid is in Mexico City. She finished the orthogonal canalisation scheme. She called me to bless the karst and serpents.' Zoe and Ursula fumed but were secretly relieved.

Sigrid, with bated breath, poured the last of the pink concrete, careful not to drip it into the Pacific Ocean. There! Het Esmildred-Sigrid-Ursula-Zoe-Lagarfljótsormurinn Orthogonale Kanalisatieschema d.w.z. Olifantgracht was finished! A school of orcas turned up. 'Go away!' Sigrid shouted. 'If you enter the canalisation scheme you will never make it back to the ocean alive!'

Ursula gazed out over the continent. She watched the first barges turn at radii perfectly suited to right angles and sighed with happiness. The orcas said, 'we could do that.'

Esmildred and Het Monster van Loch Ness tried to catch apples with their teeth but Esmildred didn't have any teeth and Het Monster van Loch Ness had a limited range of motion especially with so many cyclists giddily crossing bridges. By now the orcas were nearly in tears.

Zoe said, 'I suppose you would like me to ask what's wrong.' The orcas cried, 'Waren verveeld!' Zoe wanted to say, no, you're not but asked instead if they knew where the Netherlands were, and they said of course they did, they were Papuan and naïve enough to love decoration. It would be a long way, but they could bring her home. She said that had nothing to do with it, and they all set off.

TAKE THE
MONEY
HONEY

LUCY
ELLMANN

A guy in England recently beat up his wife on their wedding night. But he had a reason: she'd asked him to help her take off her wedding dress. I guess foreplay's a thing of the past.

Look, haven't we all had just about enough of men's idea of a good time? Porn, nuclear bombs, radioactive waste? Drones, beheadings, the *Bullingdon Club*? Factory farming? Polluting every available body of water – and then *charging* you for a bottle of drinking water! Soon they'll be charging us for AIR too, the air they've filled with toxic petrol fumes, stone dust, asbestos and nanoparticles, as well as smoke from all their stupid factories and cigars and knee-jerk barbecues.

Them and their goddam Industrial Revolution, which at school was spoken of with such reverence! The Industrial Revolution destroyed the ozone over a mere two hundred years, so now we get record droughts and floods and hurricanes and blizzards, and walruses have nowhere to lay their heavy heads. All to enable a few myopic priapic bullyboys to make a mint.

The pesticides, the herbicides, the homicides and murder suicides! School shootings. Institutional racism. Institutional sexism. Freemasonry. Online backgammon. Leaf-blowers. Diabolo chicken wings. Breweries, micro-breweries, whoppers and sliders, nanobytes and gigabytes and tetrabytes – men like anything that's either *really big* or *really small*. I wonder why.

Then there are the beards, the neckties, the neon trainers, the billions of football scarves and football shirts and baseball caps and baseball games (along with their billionaire sponsors). The dissertations of Spider Man comics fans. Men's lust for uniforms and rules and regulations. And embezzlement and tax breaks. These pursuits come in tandem with their willful and ruinous indifference to women and fear of women's bodies: menstruation, gestation, parturition and lactation, and all that yucky female stuff that is actually essential to mammalian survival, which Spider Man (surprisingly) is not. What would become of us all if *men* had to breastfeed? When there's so much pinball to be played, so many noteworthy trains coming and going, so many gun barrels to be oiled? Babies would starve.

And the sausages, the SAUSAGES! Along with all the sausage-shaped pens, cigars, trains, missiles, skyscrapers, and about a million penile towers. (Let's quickly pass over the so-called Sage Gateshead concert hall in Newcastle, which sags, spent, forever detumescing.) The globe is littered with equestrian statues, hedge funds, gold futures, and subprime mortgages. Who thought these up?

Men. Along with mafia rings, cement feet, arms deals, urban blight, crack cocaine and election fraud. Not to mention their *fetishes*, for steak, stamps, stationery, the soiled undies of schoolgirls, coins, butterflies, tool-kits, rare brands of shaving cream, antiquarian ephemera, electronics, *more* electronics, unbelievably expensive hi-fi set-ups, tobacco, apps, abs, six-packs, quantum theory, ornithology, lad mags, plasma TVs, Mahler, Wagner, the Simpsons, and Bob Dylan. Also, those really drab khaki-coloured fisherman's vests they wear, with all the pockets.

We're dying over here, man! We're snoring in the aisles and you don't even notice! I'm particularly tired of having to listen to them all play the guitar.

Them and their capitalism and their corporations and their conniptions and philosophical convictions. Their nihilism, their defeatism, their elitism, their stupid *stupid* optimism, their love of apocalypse, and all the other huge fatal male cop-outs, all the crummy ideas we've had to stomach for five thousand years while men barely acknowledged that women even EXIST.

They have proved themselves *apocalyptically* unfit to govern. Women would do a better job with their hands tied behind their backs (which, of course, they often are).

Why *do* women work for men? Not only that, but now we twerk for them too! Look at us, traipsing abjectly around our polluted earth, planning the supper. Always trying so hard to be nice. And having to *beg* for a few measly reproductive rights, or just a little help with the dishes. Poking our puny pink parasols up at the glass ceiling. It's so demeaning – especially when you're twerking at the same time.

Women now bring home the bacon and *cook* it too. Men praise us for our autonomy, which leaves them free to watch their requisite ten hours of porn a day, decide on gender quotas, and pollute rivers.

But why should women work, why should we pay for anything, when we've been robbed blind for centuries? And I mean blind. Nigella Lawson settled for some depressingly tiny divorce deal, and left old Saatchi, a publicly recognised wife-beater, wallowing in his billions. This is no way to behave!

Let's just forget equality, okay? It's dopey. It's insane! EQUALITY DOESN'T WORK, it's a half-measure. This is an *emergency*. We've got to think big. To redress sexism, end violence against women, stop bombing campaigns, and avert the coming ecological catastrophe, women need to get their hands on the reins, and fast. In fact, forget the reins, just grab the cash!

Land and property ownership is an idiotic and injurious idea, but if the world must be owned by anyone, let it be owned by women. Once in charge, women can institute a system of *common* ownership – amongst women and animals, that is. Men can have a beer allowance.

If men won't cough up the dough voluntarily, and they won't, I suggest a well-coordinated, worldwide strike by women. Iceland had a women's strike in 1975, and the whole place ground to a halt. The *trains* stopped running – and women didn't even drive the trains.

A global women's strike could take many forms. A housework strike, a labour strike, a sex strike. Maybe throw in a driving strike, since women are the unpaid couriers of the world (and cars will kill us all in the end). We could also have a lipstick and high heels strike, a pole-dancing strike, a grilled cheese sandwich strike, and strikes involving zero tolerance of golf, beef, and for god's sake, drumming. Of almost equal importance would be a giggling and simpering strike, a moratorium on the female smile. This would alarm men no end – they're so used to women smoothing things over with false cheer.

A sex strike seems *long* overdue (amongst straight women, that is – lesbians can do whatever they want). The problem with men is, they think sex is for them. Let's get this straight, once and for all: sex is for WOMEN! Throughout nature, it's *female* pleasure that counts. The multiple orgasm tops anything men can come up with.

The sex strike worked for Aristophanes' Lysistrata. Once she got all the women holed up in the Acropolis together, the men caved. Of course, many of the women wavered along the way. It takes a lot of solidarity to bring this sort of thing off – but think of the rewards! A global withholding of sex, just for a *week*, and we'd be sitting pretty. (At any rate, it's a perfect answer to any suspension of abortion rights.)

The aim of the strikes is to get men to pay us what we're owed. Not just money. We're owed orgasms, we're owed world peace. I know, I know, I sound like Miss America when I start talking about peace. Hey, they owe us for *that* too, all those beauty contests we've had to sit through! And John Wayne movies. Men owe us for all the lip-smacking, wolf-whistling, cat-calling, ass-pinching, gun-slinging, cigar-smoking, cotton-picking and gas-guzzling that's ever gone on.

They should pay us back for their belittlement of women; for their vulgarising of sex; for prostitution; for the invention of the phone, the TV, the camera, the gun, the car, the airplane, the internet, nuclear power, lipo-suction, and tanning salons. *Pay* for the low percentage of rape convictions. *Pay* for the cyclones and forest fires, the poisonings from heavy industry, world wars, and the atom bomb. *Pay* for the gas chambers, animal extinctions, child soldier indoctrinations. *Pay* for Hitler, Mao, Christopher Columbus, Trump and the Ku Klux Klan. Why not? Why *shouldn't* they pay... and pay? They can pay for the five-thousand-year-long pay gap too.

Once women own the land and the property and all the rest of it, we can start reversing the obtuse destructiveness of men. During this transition period, by the way, we won't need any male carping, thanks. They're always so *critical*, jeez. So a three-year ban on the male voice in public will be essential. Women will need time to think about how to *fix* this mess.

But it's not enough for well-meaning men to offer women their money. Women have got to *take* the money, and without shame. Why even show gratitude? *It's our money!* We and our female ancestors earned it – the hard way.

So take the money, honey. And let's have no neg-head downer shit about being a kept woman or something. That sort of consideration is a luxury of the past. This is no time for self-doubt, self-abnegation or autonomy. No time to go Dutch on dinner, or share the mortgage repayments. The world's going to hell in a hand basket, and something's got to be done about it! (Something's got to be done about that 'hand basket' expression too.) The time has come for all good women to peacefully plunder. Yanking cash from male hands is a humanitarian gesture. It's your new job, it's your right, and it's our only hope.

TAKE THE MONEY HONEY.

Don't sing for your supper, sing for *yourself*, as Bizet's Carmen would say – okay, bad example, since Carmen was killed by her jealous boyfriend. Ah men. They love to have the last word, even in operas.

We will of course have to battle against some pretty powerful mind games. For instance, we've been bullied for centuries into believing there's something wrong with being branded a 'whore'. What a clever male trick *that* was, when whores had it right all along! Not in terms of contorting your own sexuality or risking your life to please *men*, but in terms of TAKING THE MONEY.

Why are we still trying to figure this out? *Men* can't handle money! Look what they do with it: Harley Davidsons, Doc Martens, vintage railway rides, dog-racing... Men are crazy. They're always calling *us* crazy, but men are completely off the beam. They must have lost the plot some time ago. You can tell by all the wild swimming, tornado-chasing and giant vegetables.

Now, there may be a tricky interval there during the matriarchal redistribution of wealth, when newly rich women will be bombarded by lounge lizards, murderers, rapists, thieves... *So what else is new?* Just be strong, sisters. Never mind the names they'll call us, their pathetic pleas and hard-luck stories, the sure-thing investment opportunities, the physical and emotional blackmail, and all the other forms of backlash which will inevitably ensue, once men realise they're broke. Just be brave and take the moolah. It is only a matter of waiting it out. Once worldwide matriarchy is firmly established, women will at last be adequately safeguarded against male petulance. (Just being safeguarded against male decor decisions would be progress.)

So TAKE THE MONEY, and take it proudly – you've nothing to lose but your chains and your poverty and your unheard voice and your unpaid domestic labour and your painful stilettos and time-consuming beauty treatments, and about a trillion mother-in-law jokes.

Just TAKE THE MONEY. It's not prostitution, it's your civic duty. Take it for Carmen's sake, take it for Nigella, take it for that English bride still stuck in her wedding dress. Take it for the powerless, so that you can one day empower *them*. Take it for your daughters. Take the money. Take the money and run! Take men for a ride, take them to the cleaners. Take the house, take the kids, take the cake!

(And for godsake, take the Pill while you're at it, or something equivalent. Human overpopulation is the biggest threat to the natural world and, let's face it, motherhood is for the birds. If it weren't for instinct, peer pressure, faulty contraceptives and an idle hankering to reread old children's books, nobody would ever procreate.)

CATHERINE MARSHALL

THE GRAMMAR OF LEAVING

When you leave, I'll still be there
Left of centre, right of care
Where leaves are growing underfoot
Just one leaf taken from my book

A has-been, left in the ground
The surface scratched and without sound
But there is still room to grow
Through the bricks and mortar of tomorrow

But perhaps you don't know the grammar of leaving?
Because it is so:

I leave
I have left
I have been left
I will be leaving
I am going to leave
I would have left
I will leave
I left

EX ARBORETUM

Coded in the language of trust
signed, sealed and delivered
in a way that is touching
but at the same time blunt

A whitewashed kiss
not of affection
but a polite request
for an imminent X it

Now an X isle
in a sea of cheap hoardings
and highly-strung scaffolding
left with an exit, but no bow

LAS
ABUELAS

SUZY
ROMER

95

I have long since avoided mentioning what we are having for lunch in Spain if it involves sandwiches or salads because that is not real food. I hear children say, 'What's for lunch?' to their mums outside school in Logroño each day and the answers never cease to amaze me: 'Green peas and chicken in breadcrumbs,' 'artichokes and salmon fillets,' 'lentils with chorizo'. Do they just make it up? Often, both parents work, the children go to school and have various after school activities, but they still (apparently) eat two-course cooked meals at lunch time and dinner... And don't forget the sparkling flat which is apologised for if there is such a thing as an unwashed cup in the pristine kitchen sink... Well, what's going on?

Las abuelas, is the answer. These are the grandmothers of Spain, who were Franco's other army, conscripts from birth, women predestined to keep society going on a day-to-day and birth-to-death basis while Franco organised his horrors. The *abuelas* of Spain are a unique social group because they are the last women to grow up and live adult lives under Franco's dictatorship. Born before 1957, they were at least 18 years of age in 1975 when Franco died. What makes women educated under Franco different from subsequent generations? Everything.

The level to which they were indoctrinated to put every family member's needs before their own is truly astounding and still reverberates. Church, state and family instilled in these women an almost pathological duty to look after other people before themselves. Reading was frivolous, resting was lazy and considering one's own needs was selfish so all of these things were simply eliminated. As little girls they were their mothers' helpers. When they weren't at school, they looked after siblings and learned how to cook, clean, sew and, if they were in a village, look after farm animals. In my mother-in-law's family house, the animals lived on the ground floor and the family lived upstairs. The daughters helped to cook potatoes and beetroot on the stove and mash them up in a stone basin for up to three pigs at a time. They fed the hens and rabbits twice daily. They fetched water from the village fountain in clay *botijos* with two mouths for pouring.

Most girls were not expected to get more than a basic education and job choices were limited. Even the ones who got a higher education and a good job almost uniformly gave up paid work as soon as they had children. The rest of their lives were then devoted to cleaning the house, mending clothes and providing unending supplies of home-cooked food, as well as looking after the young, the old and the sick.

One *abuela* I know gave up a well-paid job so she could accompany her husband to the towns where he was sent to work as a teacher. She kept the house and brought up their three children. Later on she had enough paid work to qualify for state healthcare through some years of illness. If she hadn't worked outside home, she would still have received medical attention, but it would have been funded through her husband's social security contributions. She told me her story one afternoon as we watched her grandson and my son playing together after school. She said, 'I sometimes wonder why I gave up my career, it was such a good one,' as if it was a personal fault or an error of judgement, but the social pressure on her generation is difficult to overstate. It just wasn't done.

My friend Teresa, now an *abuela* herself, has two sisters and two brothers. She gave up a permanent job as a social worker to support her husband in his career and bring up their two children. She never regretted it. Her parents wrote in their will that they required their daughters to look after them in their old age. Nothing was required of the sons. The women of the family nursed the father until his death. Then Teresa looked after her mother in her own family home for twelve years. When her mother died, her sisters clubbed together to buy a thank you present. It was for her brother. It was an engraved watch, to recognise the time he had given on occasion, running errands for his mother.

My husband's mother loved reading as a child. She was top of her class in her village and dreamt of becoming a teacher but this was not to be. She applied to become the telephonist at the village post office, but a girl with connections beat her to it. In the end, she went into service and worked for a woman who instructed her on how to make *croquetas* from a seat by the window and then got irritated because they turned out better than her own. When she got married and had children, she worked intermittently in different jobs, not because she wanted to work outside home but because it was financially necessary. Over many years she looked after her father and both her husband's parents who came to live in her home. After their deaths, with her children grown up and gone, her husband lost his sight and developed a number of other health problems which required her care and attention.

When she made enquiries about a pension, she was told that she fell short of a contributory pension in her own name by ninety days and that it was not possible to make up the difference in social security payments. Instead, she qualified for a 'widow's pension' which is calculated as a percentage (normally 52%) of her husband's pension. Many other women are like her, and unmarried women who do not meet minimum working time requirements qualify for a small 'non-contributory' pension. The very names of the pensions make them sound like some sort of extra kindness on the part of the state, rather than recognition of the vital work such women have contributed to society. How much money did the state save on care? The abuelas were preconditioned to reject paid work unless it was unavoidable. They had their intellectual and professional dreams devalued, dismissed and replaced by an unending duty to others. They were taught to maintain the invisible substance of society and then found their own part in it was invisible.

During and after the Spanish Civil War, hunger and poverty raised the stakes of family survival to a red-alert level that ingrained itself in the nervous system and subconscious of a generation. In times of scarcity, it was a nearly impossible task for mothers to fulfil their roles as providers of food. Nowadays Spanish people joke that lentils infested with worms used to cost more than the clean ones because they contained more protein. Family qualms about consuming them were avoided by pureeing the food before serving. But dark humour only goes so far in the face of the poverty and desperation that informed people's behaviour in this period. During the Civil War, my husband's grandfather saw a man swipe bread out of another man's hand and laugh as he ate it. The other man drew a knife and slit the bread in his throat.

Hunger or the threat of imminent hunger was so scarring for the post Civil War generation that neither the arrival of money nor excess food supplies did much to change the life-or-death mission of many women to keep their families full to capacity with home-cooked food. Right up to today it isn't even a question of hoarding tins and jars because the food is not safe until it is in the bellies of the family. Depending on the dish, abuelas are barely present at the dinner table because they are finishing off the cooking as you eat each course to ensure the food is freshly cooked and piping hot. Abuelas always serve their own food to everyone to make sure the servings are big enough. There is no such thing as leftovers, even if there is enough to provide a full meal for later. Either they make triple quantities for Tupperware takeaways or they distribute remaining food on the plates of the company, saying something like, 'Just one more each and it's done.' Young people particularly are told to eat more because they are still growing.

There is a whole series of stock responses to ensure that no one at the table eats less than their personal maximum. At the time of cooking, doubts about large quantities are fielded with, '*Luego eso se queda en nada*'; 'It reduces to nothing .' (As if the food might evaporate.)

'That's too much meat' is answered with, '*Es todo hueso*'; 'It's all bone.' (It isn't.)

'That's too much rice/stew,' is answered with, '*Es plato único*'; 'There's only one course.'

Pre-ordered requests for small portions can be headed off by serving a large portion and saying, 'Do you want this much... or more?' This is particularly effective as the moment of confusion can be used to pop in another spoonful.

It may be a feature of my family-in-law only, that when my mother-in-law says, 'The *croquetas* have hardly been touched!' then one by one, each family member says, 'Well I've had three,' 'And I've had two,' and so on, in a confessional chain before the plate is handed around for more helpings. Having come from an Edinburgh family where the food is put on the table and people help themselves, this ritual has a stressful, competitive quality that makes me feel under pressure to eat more than is wise, but I am learning to appreciate that it is a question of survival. On one occasion at a friend's house, I had my hand slapped TOWARDS the food by his mother after I decided I could give the biscuits a miss at the end of an almighty home-cooked banquet. It makes me realise how fortunate British people were to have rationing in the 1940s and 1950s when other countries had so much less – though the limitless sugary treats that my Scottish granny lavished on me as a child may have been the result of her own subconscious reaction to wartime cake and biscuit privations.

To ensure that the younger generations eat well enough in terms of quality and quantity during the working week, *abuelas* prepare Tupperware boxes of food for freezing. If the son or daughter lives in another city, the *abuela* either gives them food to take back with them or actually goes to visit and spends a whole day cooking mass quantities in their kitchen. The flat probably gets cleaned while she's at it. My husband and I once visited a recently divorced man who showed us round his tacky new bachelor pad and then revealed his proudest possession: an enormous freezer containing a drystane dyke of Tupperware ready-meals prepared by his mother. For him there was no connection between his recently amplified free time and the need to cook anything for himself. I know another young man who has lunch in Logroño each day and then drives back to his village every evening. When he sees his granny, she asks him what he had for lunch and then tells him if he has eaten 'real food' or not. Tapas don't count.

If hunger is Enemy Number One then dirt is not far behind. There are good reasons for paying scrupulous attention to hygiene in a hot climate. (It is no coincidence that Spanish funerals usually take place within 48 hours of death.) Food must only be taken out of the fridge for immediate consumption and you cannot leave fruit out in a bowl in the summer months or it will go off within hours. Mouldy food and dusty corners are beloved places of flies, moths, worms and cockroaches so any remiss housekeeping can have swift and revolting consequences. The *abuelas* come from villages where farm work and animals made the task of cleaning all the more constant and demanding. They continue to maintain meticulous levels of hygiene in their flats today. There is never a thing out of place, nor any sign remaining of how this tidiness is accomplished. Leaving a bottle of washing-up liquid standing by the kitchen sink is as unthinkable as leaving the Hoover out when guests arrive because it's the sign of an unfinished job. The only place for washing up equipment (detergent, rubber gloves, scrubbing sponges) is tucked away below the sink in a neat plastic compartment attached inside the cupboard door. This secret compartment is present in every Spanish home.

Today's *abuelas* moved to towns and cities when they married because the Spanish economy was growing and there were jobs to be found in factories and shops. Since the population of Spain is largely squeezed into the coastal and river areas of the country, space is at a premium and most people live in flats. It means that no matter how rich or poor people are, the essential language they use to refer to home is the same: our flat. This adds a note of equality to conversations, even if the words do not reveal the full extent of the differences, in reality. People talk about interior and exterior windows, the stairwell and the neighbours, who are never far away because the walls are like Chinese silk screens compared to the brick or stone walls of Scotland.

You have to watch out if walking in the streets of Logroño at around 8 or 9 o'clock in the morning. If you don't keep an eye on the windows and balconies of the flats above, you may get a sprinkling of dust and dirt on your head as women shake brushes, dusters, rugs and sometimes even dust pans out of the window. Most women wait for a moment if you are directly underneath but it's as well to be careful.

This public expulsion of dirt took on a competitive edge in the village where my husband grew up. Since the shaking of the tools marked the end of the morning chores, and the speed at which these were accomplished reflected your efficiency, women would keep an eye on who finished first. Teenagers heading home at 7 or 8am after a normal Spanish night of partying would stop to pick up some bread at the baker's for their parents while the *abuelas* shot appraising glances at each other across the street as they cleaned their household tools. This is not unlike the pointed display of Scottish women of the past, vying to ensure that their front step was cleaner than anyone else's.

The reward for such unending labour was the status of the *abuelas* in their families, which was curiously high in Northern Spain, perhaps especially in La Rioja, Navarra and the Basque Country. While tasks were starkly divided between male and female work, women were often respected as the highest authority and decision makers for matters of the home and family. But these women were not charming, blushing Angels of the House, like those described and rejected by Virginia Woolf in her essay 'Professions for Women'. Slippers as projectile weapons seem to have been a common element of family life. Husbands may have escaped the slipper but no one was spared a telling-off and, if we trust the collective memory, they did not answer back. Spilling food on clothes was and is a particularly heinous crime, because it simultaneously involves wasting food and staining fabric.

There's a Northern Spanish joke about a man showing off to his friend that he always has the last word in an argument; when the friend asks what it is he says it is 'Yes, darling.' I have seen the president of a company quail as he remembered he had forgotten to tell his wife whether he would be back for lunch or not. He then stopped proceedings to phone her in very apologetic tones. My husband never speaks to his mother until after he has shaved and dressed properly, which fascinates me because this includes phone calls. When I say she won't know what you look like, he says solemnly, 'She might ask.'

Traditional mothers are also famously recognised for their ability to reconstruct the previous hours' actions of any family member by smell, when she kisses them. You get two kisses in Spain so there is ample time to notice smoke, perfume, alcohol, or other telltale signs of nefarious activity. If the FBI employed *abuelas*, there would be no need for lie detectors and lengthy interrogations. Enquiries could be accomplished with a knowledgeable glance, a light sniff and a couple of precision questions.

Many *abuelas* are still active members of the team looking after the whole family on a day to day basis. I meet a lot of them at my son's school because they pick up their grandchildren, supervise them while they play and take them home for lunch or dinner. *Abuelas* continue to do much of the work they always did because their daughters now have full time jobs. Some schools offer dinner and extra-curricular classes so children are looked after and some people have paid child-minders, but the question of childcare remains complicated. Many people live in the same stairwell as their mothers, so a huge part of the cooking and childminding gets shared out. Other couples have a cleaner, although not as many as would like. As my baker once said wryly, 'The "woman who cleans my house" is me.'

Idealised Spanish mothers still strive to achieve everything the *abuelas* did while working full time outside the home. But this impossible model is already buckling under the weight of reality and women's collective voices are demanding change. On International Women's Day in Logroño, the statues of illustrious men from history around a fountain in the city centre are usually adorned with aprons. In 2018 the slogan was 'If we women stop, the world stops.' Many women went on strike and events were organised in two hundred places in Spain with the biggest ones taking place in Madrid, Barcelona and Valencia. The issues at the fore included the pay gap, job insecurity, unemployment, pensions, femicide and male violence against women (*violencia machista*, a more accurate term than the euphemistic 'domestic violence'). The invisible work ('*trabajo invisible*') of the *abuelas* was also honoured, though its true value may never be recognised until it has gone forever.

Women protested with enthusiasm and conviviality on the streets of Logroño, a traditionally conservative area. In the women's toilets at the University of La Rioja, someone has written 'Behind every successful woman is a frustrated chauvinist.' And, I would add, at least one *abuela*, if not two.

READING
CHEKHOV
IN SIDI IFNI

ELLEN
HAIR

We amble across Plaza Espana into the shadows cast by the palm trees. A couple of old men, wearing their burnoose hoods over their heads in lieu of sunglasses, seem to dream away their retirement.

We head into the lobby of the Bellevue – the receptionist and doorman remembers us from before. A few 'bonjours ça vas' are exchanged whilst passport details are transferred to the old ledger. The TV which previously beamed out 24/7 has gone. The bookcase has gone as has the pile of dog-eared books in different languages. Wi–fi rules now! I wonder if anyone ever did borrow my Maupassant short stories which remained there between visits.

The lobby gives a context to the history of the hotel and the town. Built in the 1930's to accommodate visiting Spanish dignitaries and officials the décor and ambiance of the Bellevue is fading Art Deco. The tiles in the lobby have an Iberian as opposed to Magreb design. Enlarged and framed posters of stamps adorn the walls. These were produced from the 1940s to the 1960s at the height of colonial ambitions.

Up on the roof terrace it is indeed a 'belle vue'. The Atlantic rolls and roars in. An expanse of sand and ocean stretches below. The noise of the waves bounces off the blue and white exterior walls of the hotel. Sidi Ifni is a blue and white town. The breezeblock is blue and white too. We watch the sun sink into the sea. Delicate greys and torpid pinks hover on the horizon and on the surface of the ocean. The lighthouse starts flashing and when we return to our room we are intrigued by the blue and white hues of the beacon reflecting on the bedroom wall.

A stroll across the Plaza gives a sense of Iberian grandiosity. Off Plaza Espana sits the church, the Consulate building, the administration building and the Governor General's house. Until 1969, it accommodated the Governor of the Spanish Sahara as, Spain controlled this slice of Morocco. But this spread of sand and desert scrub is a long way from anywhere.

These buildings with their art deco designs are now empty and bereft of role: this is a previously grand town centre, where no one lives, with the exception of transient guests in the Bellevue. In Europe the Bellevue would be a museum with guides to colonial aspirations, and the history and construction of the town in several languages. There would be an adjoining café, and a visitor's centre.

The Consulate building sits on the corner of 'Calle de Sub official Zabala', whoever he was. The façade is whitewashed blue and white, the windows breeze-blocked in. The church is simply abandoned; gulls sit atop the pinnacles of the old tower. The Spanish were stamping a Christian identity on the desert, as well as producing stamps. Now a family seems to live in the former priest's house, judging by the children's laundry and plants peeking out of the windows on the way up the redundant bell tower. The mosque in a parallel side street is still used. It has the ubiquitous whitewashed walls with blue geometric patterns on the minaret. Despite its lower status and location, the mosque endures. The dawn call to prayer is a good alarm clock. 'Get up', prayer is better than sleep. The muadhan can sing too!

The central park – everything radiates off from here - has the same sense of slow decay. The palms cast shadows in the sun. The old chipped park benches have Iberian insignia and motifs, a Spanish flag and an eagle still visible.

The adjacent street houses the Art Décor Cinema Avenida. Round the corner a faded sign above a door with a 30's façade says 'Twist Club'. Strains of Sam Cooke hit my brain. No one has twisted any nights away here since Sam was murdered circa 1964. The cinema doesn't look like it has shown any films since round about the same time. A glance through a niche in the padlocked door of the Twist club reveals a roof which has fallen in. Amidst this and the other detritus a tree is growing. I fantasise about doing my own impromptu twist round the tree.

Off the esplanade with tired and faded light blue and white painted balustrades on the way down to the beach is Calle Del Colonel Portillo intersected by Calle Tetuan. The Moroccans have retained the dark blue and white Spanish street signs. It's incongruous, converging as they do with the major thoroughfare, rue de Mohammed V, where the signage is in Arabic and French. Meanwhile two downtown streets which go nowhere claim to be Calle Toledo and Calle Oviedo respectively.

My guidebook says Sidi Ifni was formerly known as Santa Cruz del Mar Pequenta, and that the place 'adds a dash of Gabriel Garcia Marquez to the usual Moroccan tagine'. I'm not so sure, besides I'm reading Chekhov. I find this town more than a dash Chekhovian. He would have identified with the provincial and melancholic languor of Sidi Ifni, and its many contradictions. We could be in Yalta.

I transpose "Lady with A Dog" to the Spanish Sahara of the 1930s. Anna and her Pomeranian walk down the grand esplanade and meet Dmitri at the beach.

They'd previously have nodded to each other over breakfast in the dining room (now unused) of the Bellevue. Anna is escaping her loveless marriage, Dmitri the eternal philanderer is looking for another attractive woman in a colonial outpost. In the evening they would observe the sunset from the terrace of the Hotel Bellevue, whilst sipping palo cortado.

Soon they will sail back to Madrid from the old port (abandoned too now) for the story to continue – love and loss. But first Anna and Dmitri (or should they have Spanish names?) could while away an afternoon matinee at the Cinema Avenida.

THE
BIN
SHED

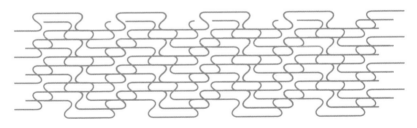

KYLIE
GRANT

Crisp packets (especially Monster Munch). Plastic bottles. Glass bottles. Irn Bru cans. Coke cans. Energy drink cans (these were the worst kind, with their sickly smell and likelihood to be left balancing on kerbsides, half full). Takeaway food containers (the squeaky polystyrene kind). Receipts. Laces. Pizza boxes. Tins. Unused dog poo bags. Used dog poo bags, tied to hedges or nestled in grass verges (Marie once saw a perfect pyramid of bulging bags and was horrified both by the rigidity of the structure and the thought that it would probably outlast her). Cigarette packets. Cigarette butts. Condoms. Sticky substances. Socks. Matted hair. Large, empty cans of cooking oil. Yoghurt pots. Sweet wrappers. Shrivelled balloons. Hair bands. String. Rope. Plastic sheeting. Plastic bags. Plastic packaging. Plastic spoons, knives and forks. Plastic lids. More plastic bottles. Plastic shrapnel. Plastic straws. Tiny plastic pots. Tampons.

Reams and reams and reams of litter, spilled out of rammed bins, lying in gutters, stuffed in hedges, stubbornly sat at the side of the road, in the middle of the road, in the way, out of the way, hidden, or in full view of everyone.

§

Early on a murky Sunday morning, Marie and a woman she didn't catch the name of were picking litter down a quiet road on the Southside of Glasgow. The area was mostly residential with red stone tenements on either side and cars parked almost on top of each other lined the road. There were also a couple of independent cafes, a tiny beauty parlour and an uninviting gift shop called Tracey's Treasures where Marie, one particularly patriotic day, bought a tartan patterned candle which she instantly regretted. There were some concessions to nature, with hedges and small areas of grass out front (some better tended than others). In fact, the road was home to one of Marie's favourite gardens, all wildflowers, hanging baskets and an uplifting number of small wind turbine replicas that whizzed in the wind. It was Marie's first litter pick and she wore a high-vis vest she had bought on eBay. She was, and looked, earnest. She walked slightly behind her designated co-litter picker. The leader of the Southside Scrubbers (Marie had never been a fan of alliteration) thought it best for the group to pair up, which hadn't bothered Marie, but had obviously annoyed her partner, who introduced herself with a nod, a half smile and a remarkably powerful handshake but not, for some reason, her name. Marie decided not to inquire further, choosing instead to call her Petra because her long braid and pinched face reminded her of a girl she went to school with. To Marie, this all felt an awful lot like school.

After collecting their litter pickers and a broom, Petra was tasked with collecting recyclables; Marie the landfill. Petra headed off around the corner, careful to avoid the other group members while Marie followed dutifully behind her. Marie was glad she had Petra because no one really said anything about where to go and being still quite new to the area she was anxious about getting lost. Petra led them down to the bottom of a long road and said that they should start to work their way up and hopefully meet back up with the group. Marie, half listening, saw a fast food container, grabbed it with her litter picker and moved to drop it into Petra's open bag. Petra moved quickly to close it but the container slipped in and sat stubbornly at the lip of the bag until she scooped it out and placed it carefully in Marie's bag instead.

'That doesn't go in recycling. Not all plastics are the same, don't you know that?'

'Oh, yes, of course. I'm sorry, I just wasn't thinking.'

'Best if we work alone. It's not you, it's just that this is the only time I get to myself,' Petra said as she took another bag out of her back pocket and walked to the other side of the road. Marie, though a little hurt, made no move to follow her, focused as she was on collecting a load of coffee cup lids and plastic bottles that were lodged in between some cars and the kerbside. She no longer believed that much was recycled any more anyway (if it ever was). In fact, in the first meeting she had managed to get with Tom, he had told her the vast majority of recycling just went to landfill because they couldn't afford the people to separate and sort it. She was so incensed that she walked out of the meeting without saying a word, only to get so lost in the rabbit warren of the council building that she ended up having to call Tom to escort her out.

She now knew quite a few things about the council's waste strategy. Tom, with his pink cheeks and tidy teeth, had always been forthcoming with information, even before he kissed her in the bin shed as she was trying to explain to him how dire the situation was with her tenement's bins. He was also the reason she was litter picking, having emailed her about the group and encouraged her to put her anger to good use and perhaps make friends with people who had an equal disdain for the state the city was in. Despite his patronising tone, she signed up immediately but did not reply to his email. Two days later, he emailed again and gave her the number of a man who he said could sort out her bin shed. She laughed when she read it, for it was not two months earlier that yet another man (a kind man who had helped move her furniture up to her third floor flat) had provided her with Tom's number saying, 'He'll sort you out; he's head of all the bins.' All these well-connected men and yet still the world was a sodding mess.

The morning mist cleared. Marie had filled two bags and could see the other members of the group in the near distance. A little earlier she had managed to pick up four cigarette butts in one go with her litter picker, but it felt like a hollow victory because Petra was too far away to be impressed. She hadn't concentrated this hard on anything since university. She wished she could go over to talk to Petra about her growing despair over just how much litter there was, but didn't want to break the peaceful equilibrium and embarrass herself further. Petra would understand though, unlike a work colleague she had tried to explain it to, who simply asked why she was so bothered, and in the grand scheme of things, was it really that bad? Yes, yes it is, she had replied. The truth was that she had recently come to the conclusion that there wasn't a particularly rational reason for why it mattered or why it angered her so much. She certainly felt that it compounded her disappointment with the whole idea of civic responsibility. However, if she owned up to this pitiably naive thought she would probably crumple like a crisp packet and be taken by the wind to god knows where.

If Marie was one to linger on her childhood, she could have easily traced her growing outrage over litter to an early dislike of untidiness. At eleven, she was so ashamed by her father cleaning their car by shovelling all of the rubbish out in the street, and then moving the car to another space to avoid detection, that she refused to get back in it for a month. In Australia, where she had lived for a short time as a girl, the streets were so clean that she cried and her mother, at a loss over what to do with her, told her that sometimes things could be too clean. Once she was bathing with her two brothers and insisted they scrub clean the tiles, grouting and taps before they could play with their pirate ship. But when younger, she had licked cat vomit off one of the plastic balls in her play pen. It tasted like crusty milk.

Until recently, though, she had not felt the urge to share her despair with others, but since her bin shed crisis she had added herself to a few Facebook anti-litter groups and while she had not posted anything herself, she excitedly scrolled through pictures of people's litter hauls. It made her feel as if things were getting done even without her, that there were people with more ambition than she would ever have. Petra was one of these people, Marie was certain of it. She watched as Petra leant down and with a gloved hand collected what appeared to be a large gathering of soggy carrier bags which had been sucked down a drain. It looked heavy and Marie crossed the road to help.

'I'm okay,' Petra said, although she smiled appreciatively when Marie held the bag open for her to deposit the dripping mess.

'Feels so hopeless, sometimes, doesn't it?' Petra said and Marie, struck by a sudden sadness, feared that if she looked Petra in the eye, she would just cry. Instead, plucking a can out of a hedge, she told Petra about her bin shed. She described the piling bags and the rotten food all over the concrete floor, the household items people tried to cram in, the endless broken vacuum cleaners, toasters and disintegrating mops.

'Ah, you need Stan,' Petra said.

'Oh, you know him too? He's coming round this morning; a friend gave me his number. Actually, what's the time?'

'Eleven. He's ex-army too so he's pretty punctual.'

§

Marie knew that tidying her bin shed before a man she'd hired to tidy her bin shed arrived was utterly ridiculous but she just couldn't help herself. I'll just move a few bags so that it is easier for him to get in, she thought as she pulled back the heavy bolt of the door to her tenement's communal garden. As always, she hesitated before she entered, trying to ready herself for the inevitable tiredness which overwhelmed her as soon as she saw what new mess had been created. This time someone had placed a broken set of drawers and a grubby mattress right by the door. Marie sighed. En route to the bin shed, but not yet inside, Marie invariably felt soft, wet mulch underfoot. She had never got to the bottom of what this was, and indeed Tom was equally baffled and refused to even hazard a guess. Spoilsport, she had said.

Marie had heard stories of bin sheds that resembled tiny stables, with small half doors to keep the bins safe and sound and clean, but hers was nothing of the sort. A sizable structure made from several long lengths of wood nailed haphazardly together, it had no roof to speak of, short of a thatch of dried and knotted tree branches and long trails of ivy, and no door. There was a concrete floor although even this was hard to make out under the mountains of black bags, discarded carrier bags and pools of bin juice. There was space inside for eight large green bins, although there were actually only five. Marie tried to move some of the bags to at least make a gangway of sorts, but the smell was overpowering. A nappy fell on her shoe and as she leant down to peel it off, her phone vibrated in her pocket.

'Mum, these calls are costing us both a fortune, can't we Skype later?'

'I know, I know it's just the time difference here makes it awkward. I like to hear about the day you've got planned. How are things?'

Marie's phone vibrated again. Stan was trying to get through.

'I can't really talk now, I've got a man coming to clean my bin shed.'

'I hope that's a euphemism.'

§

Small, stocky, and bald, Stan was exactly what Marie had imagined. Although she was disappointed that he wasn't shocked at the state of the bin shed, she felt vindicated that he had to return to his car for a thicker set of gloves. He hadn't come with many tools or in fact much equipment at all, which somewhat concerned Marie, but she soon saw that he took the job seriously when he asked about whether she had an outside tap. She had nervously paid him upfront, which eased her guilt about the fact that she was going to leave him all alone with what to her seemed an insurmountable task. He had thanked her quietly for the cash but laughed loudly at her jokes about bins.

Marie didn't want it to look like she was watching him, so she returned to her flat and tried to pretend she hadn't just paid a strange man to root around her bin shed. An hour later and she had only peeked out of the window once, where all she could see was him fixing a wheel back on to one of the bins. Once on, he spun it around and around, and although she could not see his face, she imagined it lit with glee.

Later, while she lay on her bed thinking about going down and offering Stan a drink, Marie heard the door buzzer and rushed to the intercom.

'You got a sieve, love?'

'A sieve? What for?'

'Well, there's a hamster at the bottom of one of your bins. It's floating in all the liquid but I can't seem to get at it.'

'A hamster? Are you sure it's not a rat or a mouse?'

'Nah, I know my hamsters. A beauty of a Russian Blue.'

'Is it dead?'

'Aye.'

Once downstairs, Marie passed Stan the sieve. He thanked her with real emotion.

'I didn't want to empty the bin into the drain like I usually would, you see, as then the little thing would just go straight down.'

Marie watched as he crawled into a bin that he'd taken from the shed and leant at an angle. He sieved out a tiny hamster from inside. He reached for a water bottle and wiped away the putrid liquid which covered its fur.

'Most likely some kid's mum just threw him away. They're probably still looking for him.'

'Why is it always the mum? Dads mess kids up too, you know,' Marie said but then almost immediately regretted bringing gender into it.

'Aye, you're right about that. We should bury him. Give him a proper send off.'

Marie nodded in agreement, though unsure exactly what this would entail. She followed Stan around the garden until he settled on a small patch of ground near an old cherry tree which had not produced fruit in some time. He knelt down and dug a small hole with his hands and gently placed the hamster inside. Marie joined him on her knees and refilled the hole. They both stood up and looked at the tiny mound for a few moments. The wind picked up.

'I shouldn't be too much longer.' Stan gave back her sieve. 'Just make sure you wash it, yeah?'

Marie returned upstairs, lay down on her sofa and promptly fell asleep. She woke in the early hours of the morning. She checked her phone and found a message from Stan confirming that he had finished and could he share the pictures he took on his business Facebook page. There was also a message from her mother asking if she was free for a chat and that she trusted her shed man was everything Marie had hoped for. Marie tried to go back to sleep but birds were chattering and all she really wanted to do was to see the shed. After a short while, she got up, found a torch and as quietly as possible walked down the stairs to the garden.

It was raining and she was being watched by an angry neighbourhood cat but Marie hardly noticed because before her stood the most immaculate bin shed she had ever seen. The bins were no longer half full of foul smelling liquid and now sat nestled cosily side by side. There were no bags on the ground. Not one. Not even a stray carrier bag. The floor had been washed and swept and even the mulch had gone. Some of the ivy had been trimmed or tied back. No nappies or sanitary towels were stuck to any surfaces. No takeaway containers with half eaten dinners floated in pools of water. A new notice had been strung up to remind people not to leave bags on the ground and warning them about the dangers of rodents and disease. Everywhere she looked, things had been tidied, cleaned and organised. The rain pelted down and the torch flickered. Marie stood there for some time in the dark, never having known a bin shed could be so painfully beautiful.

LET THERE BE
LIGHT

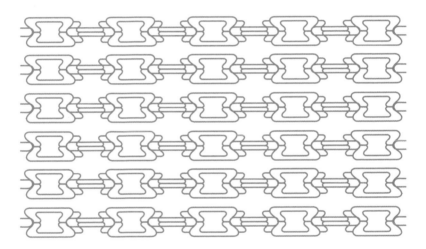

RAFAELA
TAYLOR

In the last few years City of Edinburgh Council has been selling off the city's collective heritage for short-term economic gain. I fear that while our home is being made more attractive to tourists, we are losing the places that enable our lives.

My painting focuses on the publicly owned land and NHS clinic that sit behind Edinburgh Central Library. They have been sold off to build a Virgin hotel. The library was gifted to the people of Edinburgh by the industrialist-cum-philanthropist Andrew Carnegie, who called on the rich to use their wealth to improve society.

The decision by those in power to sell the land and buildings will have lasting consequences (a 'luxury' hotel, rather than a library extension as promised, a library starved of daylight and the loss of the NHS clinic are just three...) yet it seems to have been made behind closed doors, favouring the interests of shareholders over residents' well-being.

A group of Edinburgh residents have been relentlessly trying to reverse this tragedy. The image of one activist camping up in the tree on the site before he was evicted, and the tree was cut down stuck with me for almost two years before I worked up the courage to paint this.

I have used the language of religious and classical symbolism to tell the story without words. A shadowed Carnegie presides over the phrase inscribed on the library doorway: 'Let There Be Light'. the tree of knowledge, beset by the three-headed serpent caricaturing the business owners, drops leaves and knowledge-seekers as the porcine councillors look on in glee.

There is a sense of the decline in quality since Carnegie built his fine stone library: leaves turn to money, dropping into a black hole; the impermanence of the cranes against the castle; the security pigeons making the public private, and the latest shoddy 'iconic' building referenced at the bottom – the 'golden turd' luxury hotel and shopping centre on Edinburgh's Leith Street.

Rafaela Taylor
15 May 2019

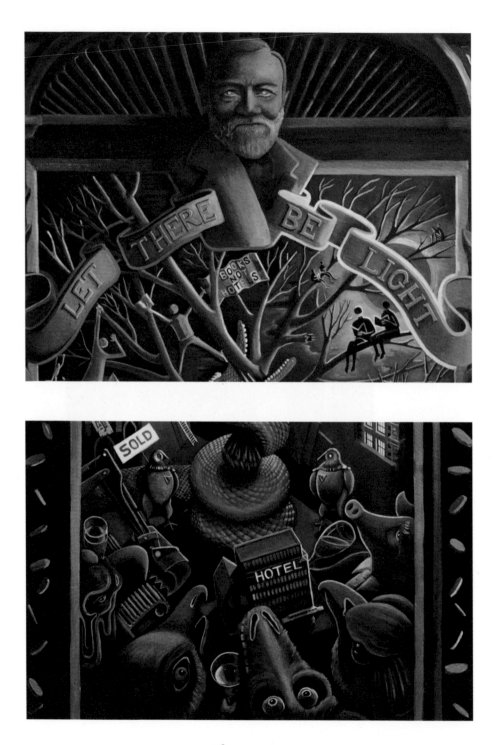

BLACK EYES

KRISTEN
LOWMAN

Maria stood alone, watching as the other children took turns beating the lamb that hung from a tree. Slowly she walked backward, unable to take her eyes off the animal that swung hypnotically, its black eyes never losing her.

With her thumbs tucked into her fists, she took another step backward and gasped. Someone had grabbed a lock of her hair. Too frightened to cry out, she jerked her head to free herself from her captor and turned. She sighed, relieved; her hair, she saw, was only caught on a branch of a bush. A very tall bush it was. Another stood to her left, towering. They had been tended, watered and pruned. Maria felt like a tiny weed standing in their shadows. Not an unfamiliar feeling. Not a bad feeling. Her small, bony fingers worked quickly like spider legs, untangling the fine, dark strands wrapped around green leaves and their wooden spines. Still caught, she began tugging, finally grabbing the stubborn strands with both hands. She yanked, ripping the hair, freeing herself.

Across the yard, boys yelled and made explosions with their lips and spit as they popped balloons. Glancing upwards into the bush, she spied a dusty, vacated web draped among its dark inner branches; within the weave of this gossamer net were the remnants of the spider's past prey fluttering desolately. A gull flew above. She'd never seen one this far inland from the Gulf where there were no garbage dumps or fish. This part of town where Andrea Jones, the birthday girl, lived had brand new houses that stretched out on wide, soft lawns. These houses seemed sleepy and lazy, unlike her windblown house with its blistered and peeling paint that looked like it struggled to stay up, her house like an old person. The gull swooped. It's a Laughing Gull her father had taught her, but there was nothing funny about being far from your home on the Texas Gulf.

Andrea Jones beat furiously with the baseball bat at the swinging creature's rear. Bits of coloured paper flew off its limp tail. One of the boys yelled, 'Stick it in him!' The girls made bad-taste-in-the-mouth-sounds and laughed. Maria noticed Andrea was no longer having fun; she was angry, determined, hearing no one, like a grownup, like Maria's father when he was 'getting the job done' on the shrimp boat. When he was 'getting the job done' on the pickup he called a cocksucker, screaming at Maria to 'hand me the god damn wrench!' She remembered his arm reaching from beneath the hood of the car, his greasy palm flapping. She'd been too afraid to ask which wrench, the big one or the little one, and so he screamed at her again.

Maria was glad she was unseen. If they made her swing at the lamb, she would kick and scream and run. If they dragged her back, she would beat them with the bat. They didn't know that she could do that.

Her hand searched for the bump at the back of her head. It was tender, squishy, about the size of her palm. She knew it came in the night, from a dream it seemed.

Slowly the paper skin began to give way, splitting, spilling candies like colored shards of bone. Andrea Jones threw the bat down and smiled, placing her hands on her hips like the gym teacher. The children, now united, screamed victoriously and ran like a mob in the movies towards the sweets and toys. They scrambled for their loot, stuffing candy in their mouths, pelting each other with gumballs, filling their pockets. One of the boys bounced on his toes with his fists held high, shouting, 'Roc-ky!' and then punched the boy next to him.

She crouched on her haunches between the bushes that bordered the Jones' garden wall, pulling her dress over her knees, and watched Oliver, who was so pale and quiet in school, flush pink and bare his teeth, growling at the girls in ruffled frocks who ran squealing helter-skelter like piglets. The girls returned for more scary fun from the bad boy. The girls, so pretty, thought Maria. She was the smallest person in the fourth grade. Her mother told her a work of art did not come quickly. Her schoolmates called her a Mexican, a Spic. She was Creole like her daddy, she told them. Same thing, they said.

Maria noticed Petey, a wiry, freckled boy, climbing stealthily up the tree and onto the limb. He reached for the rope that dangled the remains of the lamb, pulling it onto his thighs. Grabbing its head, he smashed it against the bark until it too split open. 'Nothin' in there!' He released the rope; the lamb's head fell and jerked, spinning to the left and to the right.

Petey's father was the butcher in town. Yesterday when Maria's mother asked for half a pound of hamburger, he scooped the meat onto the scale until the needle was just right and then put in a bunch more. Her mother said, 'Thank you, George.' His name, said softly and carefully, came floating as if in a bubble from her mother's mouth. Petey's father cracked no joke when he said, 'For the Yella' Rose of Texas, anything.' And then they had a slow taffy pull with their eyes. Remembering Maria, he plunged his big, scarred hand into a jar and withdrew a pickled egg. 'For the Black-Eyed Susan,' he said, presenting it to her with a paper napkin pulled swiftly from behind the counter.

In the parking lot, her mother walked ahead, gripping Maria's hand. Maria scuttled behind, taking two steps for each of her mother's one. 'Mr Baylons and I are old friends from high school,' her mother said, without looking at her. As if Maria didn't know that.

Her mother pulled open the passenger door and Maria climbed up onto the hot plastic seat.

Inside the truck, her mother said, 'Take this, honey,' and handed her the bag of meat.

The brown paper bag felt cool and round like a baby's bottom on her lap. 'How come he called me Black-Eyed Susan? My name is Maria.'

Her mother turned the key, frowning as she pumped the pedal several times like she was stepping on something alive and bad. 'Damn truck.'

'How come?'

'How come what? Oh. It's a flower, honey.' This time when the key turned the motor woke up loud and hungry. Maria nodded and bit into the rubbery egg stained pink with beet juice.

Petey bounced fearlessly on the limb – King of the Jungle – making monkey noises. One girl with blond curls had pushed a boy to the ground and was quickly pouring M&Ms down his shirt. They choked on laughter. Maria smiled, reminded of Blackie's paws pushing her to the ground playfully in the yard. Telling Blackie to 'shush, be quiet,' fearful her father would hear. Knowing her mother pretended not to.

The dog had chosen her. He had wandered lean and worn into her yard three moons ago and settled into the dirt flowerbed beneath her window to lap at the leaking water faucet. Lying still in her bed, her heart pounding, she had thought at first he was a prowler; his paws walked the ground with the weight of a man. But she recognized the harmless sound of his lapping tongue followed by his flapping ears as he scratched.

Maria slowly rose to her knees on her bed next to the window. She carefully lifted the window that was partially open, expecting him to run away, praying he wouldn't. There he was. A big black dog, his eyes shiny with moonlight. They stared at each other, neither afraid.

'Don't go,' she whispered and climbed off her bed. She grabbed a box of animal crackers from her desk, scampered back, and leaning out the window, sprinkled the tiny zoo at his feet. He sniffed unenthusiastically but ate anyway.

Maria sighed, 'Oh, Blackie.'

From then on, every night after the house was asleep, she rose, opening her window fully, closing it in the morning. She placed ferreted bits of her dinner on the sill. Food slipped into a paper napkin when her mother jumped up to check the stove or when her father, tipping back in his chair, opened the icebox to reach for another beer. Sometimes her mother, who never mentioned Blackie, tucked Maria in bed, leaving chicken livers wrapped in tin foil or a small bowl of rice with bacon fat on her desk. 'Sweet dreams, honey.'

Maria would have offered Blackie all her seashells, including her conch that when first seen in the sand, looked like a tiny white shell. Her toe had nudged and then dug, soon her heel gullied and then she fell to her knees. Digging feverishly, she pulled loose a large conch, pink and mysterious. She imagined offering it to him like a tribal chief of a tropical island, the conch held in her extended arms. He could have the prettiest beads from the old button box, her silver ring from Mexico, anything at all; he could have all her belongings if he would just belong to her.

The big black dog was smart. He had known to wait for the sounds of the Gulf spilling into the dreams of the townspeople. He always waited, his ears alert, she just knew, for the silence that carried the strain of sparkling sea foam crackling on the shore, the grinding hiss of sand as it is dragged once again into the sea.

Every night, her hands clasped as if in prayer, Maria waited on her knees by the window. She sometimes nervously rearranged the food, withholding a bone for Blackie's dessert. Sea air dampened her face lifted toward the sky and filled her room with a salty stickiness. Beyond their rusted gate was the road, ragged and gray. It cut through the land like an old scar, separating her house from the lot that held in its yellowed grass nothing but steps to where a trailer had been and disappeared. Beyond was the black sea on which stretched and winked the red, green and white lights of the shrimp boats. She would guess, choose really, which boat was the Pearl Mae and think of her Daddy out there breathing diesel as his burning hands sorted the shrimp from the fish, crabs, and garbage the outrigger had hauled up from the Gulf.

He would have been promoted to wheel watch, the job that allowed him to stare at the bobbing city on the sea, a job that had men counting on him for protection. If he hadn't found that unopened bottle of whiskey in the net. 'Johnnie Walker! A gift from the sea!' she had heard her dad cry, shutting the front door with a happy slam. Maria sat up in bed, listening in the dawn light. 'Come on, Darlene,' he said to her mother, 'what's the big fuckin' deal? Bobby Jones still got his money's worth from me.'

Maria heard her mom say nothing, just throw the car keys on the kitchen table. Who was Johnnie Walker? She imagined a shrimper's ghost rising up out of the Gulf.

But it turned out Johnnie Walker was only a whiskey name and her dad had gotten drunk, almost fired by Andrea's dad, Mr Jones, who owned the fleet of which the Pearl Mae was one. Maria knew; she'd overheard Mrs Jones in their kitchen a few days later telling her mother, 'I saved his ass, Darlene. Bobby is leanin' towards hiring some of these Vietnamese. They work cheap and don't talk back. And I'll tell ya, it's one way to keep them people from fishin' our shrimp.' Maria heard the squeak of the cabinet opening and a plate pulled down. 'You hear me, Darlene? You gotta get that husband of yours to lay off the hooch.' Her mother blew a puff of breath and said, 'Not so easy.' 'Darlene. So he can lay off you. And we both know what I'm talkin' about. I said it once, and I'll say it again. You should have married George Baylons.' Maria heard her mother's silence. 'At least you'd get a good piece of meat on the table,' Mrs Jones said, helping herself to a piece of her mother's sissy pie. 'You gotta give me this recipe.'

Waiting on her knees for Blackie, Maria's eyes pulled away from the lights on the Gulf, from thoughts of her father. Scanning the shoreline, she looked for her new friend. As if from out of the sea itself, his dark form appeared bounding across the dry empty land. Maria smiled in wonderment each time, as if at a miracle, watching as he slowed down to click-clack across the road, enter through the gate and trot to the window, his tail wagging.

Standing on his hind legs, he placed his front paws on the sill to eat. His sharp teeth bit and gently tossed the morsels to the back of his throat. Once finished, his black eyes looked up into her black eyes. Then quickly, shyly, he licked her face once. 'Your welcome,' she whispered. Leaning out her window, Maria stroked his head, scratched his ears, nothing more. Be patient, she chided gently, her mother's voice in her head.

Yawning, bleary-eyed, she refused to lie down to sleep until he had curled into himself in the flowerbed below. In the morning he was gone.

One night she awoke to see the dog asleep at the foot of her bed. Smiling in the dark, she breathed, 'Blackie.' Her small body leaned over, her belly pressing against his spine, her arms wrapping around him, one under his neck, the other around his chest. She hugged him with all herself. Blackie gurgled in his throat. She thought he was trying to say her name but she remembered she'd never told him. 'I'm Maria.'

Then she lay back, resting her head on the pillow, the dark tendrils of her hair splayed like sea anemone. She felt no need to look at him again that night; he would be returning, she knew, for as many nights as he had in him. No need to panic, to gobble up his love as if storing it for days when there was nothing; it was her father's love she grabbed at, that she bent down like a willow stick for, leaving notes in careful cursive saying, 'I'm sorry, Daddy.' Sorry for what, she didn't always understand, but that was her fault too, not knowing how to please her father. Her father, who sometimes woke her at dawn, slicking his dark hair back with both hands, smiling with a wolf's shine in his eyes. 'Get up. We're going down to the shore.' 'But I have school, Daddy.' 'Your father's gonna teach you something that school of yours can't. A lot of birds to see, baby girl.'

She could now count all the birds she knew on both hands and a foot and three toes. She bet she knew more bird names than any one else in her class – the black skimmer, the whooping crane, the harrier, the ruby throated hummingbirds who flew in like a Christmas and left, the scissortail, the piping plover. And she could spot them without binoculars, so many flying feathers.

But when she recalled these special times with her father, she liked to skip over the parts when, hungry and tired and no longer able to keep up, she watched him walk ahead growing small in the distance. He occasionally turned back to look at her, throwing his arms in the air. The part when she'd have to wait in the truck for a minute that turned into an hour while he dropped by Kitty's Place to say a quick hey, bouncing in as one Daddy and stumbling out as another, driving home all sloppy.

She shyly wedged her foot between Blackie's warm belly and the bed covers, hoping Blackie didn't mind if she touched him like they breathed together, and she heard, as if for the first time, the moored vessels off shore creaking, groaning, their mast lines clanging as they shifted in their watery beds. The waves said hush when they reached the shore. The bed pulsed with the dog's quick rhythmic breathing, rocking Maria as she stared at this second full moon that shone like an opening to a new world, and she slept.

'Maria, darlin',' called Mrs Jones from across the lawn, 'grab some goodies!'

Maria froze. Behind her was the garden wall. In front, noise and mess. There was no escaping; the red brick wall enclosed them all like a fancy prison. It was an unnatural yard that had nothing to do with the windblown twisted scrub oaks growing on the sandy, flat terrain of this stretch of Texas; had nothing to do with the cranes and pelicans Maria had seen more than once floating dead offshore, fishing line wrapped around the neck or a lure caught in the throat.

Mrs Jones, 'Marebeth' Maria's mother called her, grabbed a drink and cigarette from the patio bar before loping toward Maria. Why did grownups have to carry their drinks everywhere they go, she wondered. Her daddy couldn't hop in his pickup without a can of beer. Couldn't answer the phone without a can of beer. Couldn't yell at her mother without a can of beer.

Marebeth wore tight slacks with creases that fanned out like cat whiskers on each side of her 'down there.' A blouse was tied beneath her bosom and her stomach jiggled. Her dyed blond hair was teased so high it had nowhere else to go. Not like Maria's mother who had recently begun wearing her long honey brown hair loose and fluffy, even though Maria's father told her she looked 'like a goddam hippie.' 'Mom looks like Farrah Fawcett, Dad,' she'd said gently, 'from the TV.' Her father had stopped, his face unreadable, and then broke into a grin. 'Well, now,' he said, 'looks like I got two angels then. You and your mother.'

Mrs Jones was oblivious to the liquid sloshing over her glass as her high heels sank into the grass with each step. She looked alternately surprised and irritated.

'Maria, darlin', don't you want some goodies to take home?' Her voice was breathless and deep like a man's.

Maria shook her head.

Mrs Jones squinted, staring at her like she was looking for something tiny. Dragging heavily on her cigarette, she snorted smoke from her nose at Maria's face. 'You're just like your mother. Won't get in there and take something for yourself.'

Maria noticed Betty, her chubby face shiny with sweat, standing behind Mrs Jones. Chewing loudly on a sticky-looking blob, Betty stared with cow eyes at Maria. A red candy stain extended beyond her lips as if she had been unable to color within the lines. 'Is she in trouble?' asked the girl with a sudden gleam in her eyes.

Startled, Mrs Jones whirled around, spilling more of her drink. 'Oh, for crissake, Betty, don't sneak up on people like that. Take Maria and go join the other kids, find Andrea. Maria, go with Betty. And, darlin'? If you pretend you're havin' a good time, maybe you will.'

Betty flounced ahead, leaving Maria to trail behind. She felt Mrs Jones looking at her, shaking her head, deciding things about her. Maria lifted her chin and made herself a little taller.

There really wasn't anything left to take even if she had wanted to. The grass was strewn with wrappers, chewed and spat candy, sharp bits of crushed party favors, and the lamb lying shredded. There was something, though, that caught her attention. The black eyes of the lamb. They were in the grass, two black painted orbs on cupped, stiff, cream colored paper, looking in her direction, and for a moment she forgot Mrs Jones and the party and walked toward them. She gently lifted the black eyes and fingered them.

'Come on, kids! Time for cake!' Mrs Jones hollered.

Maria quickly placed the eyes in the pocket of her dress. Walking to the edge of the crowd of children, she decided to participate to avoid drawing attention to herself. When they sang 'Happy Birthday,' she mouthed the words.

Underneath the vine-covered patio, a Mexican lady helped Mrs Jones pass paper plates of pink and white cake. But there was a problem. They'd run out of Cokes. The boys complained louder than the girls but the girls had voices that hurt the ears. Mrs Jones slid open the glass door, yelling, 'Hold your horses! Calm down!' and stepped inside for more soda, more ice cream, muttering something about feeling like a g.d. waitress.

But Maria had nothing to eat the cake with and already her ice cream was melting. Sidling up to the table on the patio, she found a plastic fork and took a seat at the long trestle table in the yard. She carefully lifted a pink rose made of icing from the cake and slid it into her mouth, noticing the girl beside her didn't get a rose and neither did the girl across from her. Pasty and sweet, it coated her tongue and stung her teeth. Again, her hand reached for the bump at the back of her head. Tracing the spongy swelling with her fingers, then patting it, she felt there was something inside this strange egg, a secret she needed to know.

Last night as her father's dinner sat cold on the stove, Maria watched her mother smoke cigarettes, one after the other, on the back stoop. Usually when her father was away, her mother played a scratched Beatles record and knew all the words when she sang along with the Fab Four, their other name. Or while fixing dinner, her mother ran now and then into the living room to hear Walter Cronkite on the TV. Back in the kitchen, she'd shake her head as she stirred whatever was on the stove, saying, 'Oh my God, this country is in uh-oh trouble.'

But last night her mother was in trouble. The Pearl Mae had docked that morning. Yes, he'd had one too many, Kitty from Kitty's Place had said on the phone and no, nobody'd seen him leave.

Maria and her mother needed his paycheck. The last time her mother had worked he had made it so she couldn't. But later, she made Maria swear not to tell anyone, to cross her heart but not die, she was learning something called a 'word processor.' 'At the library, and it's free, Maria. And then I can make money.' Her mother, staring into her eyes, gently lifted her chin. 'Anywhere,' she said. As if Anywhere were Disneyland. Her mother, Darlene as the rest of the world knew her, reached down and hugged her so hard it hurt.

Maria pushed the plate away. She didn't want any cake. She wanted her mother. She wanted her heartbeat that she could see in her neck on a hot day. Her mother in the light, her Blackie in the night, they were her whole day. She pressed the knot at the back of her head, its ache signaled a bigger ache, a dread in her belly. And she felt a new kind of fear.

She wanted again the moonlit night, a few weeks ago, when she crawled fearlessly out her window, Blackie following. It was hot and the Gulf was close and cool. She walked to the shore, her nightie sticking to her warm skin, the sand soft under her feet.

Sinking into the water, she watched her nightie balloon around her. She looked like a jellyfish in the moonlight. On shore, Blackie paced back and forth, stopping now and then to stare at her, as if willing her out of the sea. 'I'm okay, Blackie!' she called.

She drew in a big breath and dived beneath the gentle waves. Gliding under the skin of the sea, mixing herself into its silky coolness, she looked upwards; bits of gold floated as if dropped from the moon. She drifted in the Gulf's belly, where up can be down and down can be the sky and she can move between the two like a bird with fins.

Legs kicking, she descended deeper, hearing the whining cry of life pressing in her ears, calling her back to the solid world that does not catch her when she is struck down. Her arms and legs pushed her downward and she heard her father's deep voice call faintly, 'Mari-a.' She stopped. Her feet paddled, her arms reached out. She felt a memory. Her mother's laughter rocking her in the warm water. Then darkness, creeping as her father's fingers spread, stroking her mother's taut skin, blocking out the light. 'Mari-a.'

Too far! She had gone too far down into a darker and colder sea. Her lungs stretched, aching, and her throat clenched tight, trapping this last breath from the solid world. As she propelled herself towards the moonlight, desperate for air, she loved her father as she had loved him from the beginning, as if love were her first breath. With each upward stroke and downward pull of her arms, her hair rose and fell and she soon saw waves jostling in the moonlight. She surfaced, gasping.

There he was, waiting for her.

'Blackie!' she cried joyously. On shore, he licked her salty legs and herded her back to the house. In bed, with her feet resting on Blackie, she slept with a smile on her face.

Maria heard relaxed, cheerful voices coming from the kitchen, the sound of mothers coming to fetch their children. The sliding glass door opened and out stepped women in dresses, women in slacks whose shoes clattered and scraped. Some ate potato chips from a bowl on the table, telling their children to 'get a move on.'

Hurry up, Mom, she pleaded silently. The egg on the back of her head throbbed, as if pain was hatching.

When she opened her eyes this morning, she had thought the faint smell of diesel and cigarette smoke that hung in the air was leftover dream. A bad dream had come to get her in the night. She saw, too, in the light, a web of cracks in her window that had been shut by someone – not her – shut very hard.

Her head felt like a water balloon as she opened her door and tiptoed into the hallway. She stepped quickly back into her room as her father stumbled past her in his undershorts, stinking of cigarettes and sweat that smelled like beef stew. His eyes were red and swollen and did not recognize her.

Hearing him in the kitchen, she walked noiselessly to her mother's room; Maria wanted to show her the mysterious bump on her head. Her mother would tend to her with a conclusive kiss. She slowly turned the doorknob, and her father, from the kitchen, banged the table and snapped, 'Don't go in there. Your mother's sleeping.'

Maria knew her mother would never forget to pick her up. It was she who had asked Maria to please attend Andrea Jones's party. 'For the sake of your father's job,' her mother explained. And there this morning by the telephone was Andrea's gift, a pretty bottle of bubble bath, neatly wrapped.

At noon, dressed for the party, Maria knocked softly on her mother's door but there was no answer. She nestled her face into the V of the doorjamb. 'Mom, are you still sleeping?' she whispered loudly. She had already eaten her cereal in the backyard and been to the shore looking for Blackie tracks but there were none, no trace of him. It seemed he vanished in the harsh light of the day. But at this moment it was her mother, more than anything, she wanted to see.

With one hand still on the knob and the other placed above to restrain the warped door's creaks, she pushed slowly. Suddenly she was yanked by her collar and the door slammed shut. 'I told you not to go in there!' her father yelled. 'But I have to go to Andrea's birthday party,' Maria whispered, tears filling her eyes.

'You can walk.'

She left quietly out the front door, leaving her father on the couch drinking beer and watching a ballgame on television. She was going to be late for the party because Andrea lived Maria didn't know how far away on the other side of town.

She stood in the yard waiting, listening for the pickup pulling into Mrs Jones's driveway, the squeal of the brakes, the chunky sound of the cab door pushed shut. Moments later her mother would slide open the glass door, singing, 'Hi, honey. You ready?' And later in the cab of the truck, she'd take Maria's hand and say, 'You okay?' But her mother did not come.

The sun was high in the sky, a hot hat she did not want to wear. She moved to the shade of the tree, fingering the eyes in her pocket like a rosary.

With Blackie at the foot of her bed last night, Maria stared out her window at a cloud like a small mountain range from another planet floating across the moon as she tried to find God's face in her prayers but He was far away, like a small photograph pinned to the sky. It was Blackie's face that filled the front wall of her mind. Her silent prayers asking God to please, please keep Blackie safe, and please, God, make everything okay, not knowing what okay meant but it had to do with her father and her mother and anyway, God, the grownup in the sky, would know; and also, but it wasn't real important, make her grow a little taller. She sent her words upward but they couldn't go that high and so they fell like soot behind Blackie's great face, Blackie's eyes seeing her. Blackie right there at her feet. She must have slept then with her undelivered prayers.

And then what? Diesel. The smell of diesel filling her lungs, burning her nostrils. The smell of diesel pulling her up like a puppet gasping, frightened. She looked to Blackie for protection but he was gone.

She remembered now. Pictures were coming from the egg at the back of her head. She'd leaned out the window for air. She leaned out looking for Blackie. There he was in the yard, huge in his anger, teeth bared, growling. His fur rose spiked like a suit of armor. Was he growling at her? And then she knew. Her father was behind her. She turned – he was the darkest dark in the room. 'A fuckin' dog! Now I gotta feed a fuckin' dog! What else you two hiding from me?' The growl grew louder. 'Get out of her room!' her mother screamed from the hallway. Maria turned again, gripping the sill to hoist herself up and out as Blackie ran toward the window. Her father's arms were over her, reaching for the sash, and she heard it falling, the window, too fast for her to duck away.

She felt an explosion in her head. And as she fell back she heard Blackie's head hit the window as his body slammed hard, shaking the room, and even in her confusion and pain, she was stunned that the glass did not shatter. Blackie was as silent as the screams in her throat. And she heard her father yelling as if from far away, throwing words like stones at her, words felt more than heard. She was falling through all the layers of the earth, so far down that surely she would be greeted by a Chinaman at the other end.

She awoke to a banging sound against her wall, it beat rhythmically, steadfastly; she imagined a buoy against a boat. She knew her house was not a boat. The sound was coming from her mother and father's room, the other side of her wall. She heard her mother cry 'No!' and tried to sit up but the pain in her head threw stars at her and the bad dream returned. She dreamed Blackie was gone, and it was her fault he was lost to her, lost to this house where he could no longer sleep.

No trace of the party remained. The Mexican lady, having worked around Maria, entered the house, shutting the door behind her. Maria wondered, was she really in the yard at all, and checking, lifted her feet to see the impressions of her shoes in the grass.

She sat in the shade beneath a tree, the shade as good as water, and leaned against the trunk, still fingering the eyes. Hearing the door slide open, she turned. Mrs Jones stuck her head out. 'For lord's sake, come inside, Maria! Let me call your mother.'

Maria stood up. Her heart was beating fast. She didn't want her to call her mother. She didn't know why but she didn't. 'That's okay. She's picking me up at The Dairy Queen. We're going to have ice cream together.' She'd seen the happy red and white sign on her way to the party.

'More ice cream?' she asked, as if Maria was a big pig like Betty. 'Suit yourself. Did you get your party favor?'

'Yes,' Maria lied for a second time. 'Thank you.' She walked quickly to Mrs Jones whose head tilted to one side, her face scrunched up with impatience.

Inside the house was cool, the kitchen was large and clean like kitchens in TV shows with families. Mrs Jones walked her across soft carpet to the front door. 'Now just what were you doing outside if you're supposed to be at the Dairy Queen?'

Her heart was still beating quickly. Loud and fast. There was another heart in her egg; it too beat loud and fast. 'Oh. I fell asleep.'

Opening the door, Mrs Jones stopped and looked down at her. 'Honey, you need to wake up.'

Maria walked the two blocks to the Dairy Queen, to make the lie true. She almost believed her mother would meet her there.

She found a picnic table under the corrugated awning and sat facing the road. She would hear the truck coming before she saw it. Maria watched the teenagers saunter up to the window to place their orders, watched them laugh and slap each other, shaking their hair in front of their faces. Parents sat at the other tables with little children eating chocolate dipped cones. Some people hurried back to their cars clutching white paper bags and drinking from big paper cups.

She was thirsty. Water was free, she remembered. But she had to ask for it and she didn't want to. But she was so thirsty. She walked shyly up to the window counter that came up to her neck; she thought she must look like a head on a plate to the pretty teenager in the red Dairy Queen dress. 'May I have a glass of water, please?'

'Sure. Anything else?' The waitress smiled at her.

'Not yet. My mother is coming.' The pretty teenager handed her a large cup with plenty of ice. 'Thank you.'

The cars in this part of town moved slowly like parade cars, gleaming and sleek, and there weren't too many, but still she moved closer to the road; that way her mother would not miss her. Sitting on the curb in the shade, she drank and chewed on ice. Sparrows hopped around the tables and chattered in the trees. One scissortail was hidden in the branches. Flies buzzed, darting in and out of the large garbage can. The teenagers in their cars pulled out, turning up their radios. She studied the grains of sand at her feet, the sparkles in the blacktop. And still her mother did not come. The sun like a hat was slowly sliding off her head.

Reaching into her pocket, Maria took the black eyes out and held them up to her own. They fit. She blinked into the darkness.

THE
GRIPPE

PHOEBE
WELLER

Our Thomas says it all began when we closed the shop early because of the Beast from the East. He says after I left he went out for a cigarette and there was Tomas sitting there begging and the snow was falling on him the way that that snow was – with so much air in it like polystyrene flecks and just piling, settling thickly on top of him. Thomas says he offered Tomas tea, then, and then a cigarette, and it began.

Tomas begs on one side of the street and his wife Jo begs on the other side. She is beautiful, he is not. They are young. Twentysomething – it is difficult to tell these days. I am getting older but all that really means is that everybody else looks younger – impossibly, peachily, cleanly young. But when Tomas opens his mouth you can see his teeth are rotten and all over the place and he is so open and every time he opens his mouth it's an argument. When he comes in to pick up sittingcardboard in the morning he doesn't open his mouth any more. He opens his rotten mouth in the evening when he comes in to change the beggingcoins into useful notes. He meows the numbers at me in Romanian, correcting my English, brusque, sharp, annoyed or not annoyed, annoyed or playing annoyance, just disconnected enough to play annoyed/not annoyed.

On the street they are solemn and solid and unmoving, playing the part of beggars, still and sad and stuck. When they change the beggingcoins into notes they are loud and joking and she laughs and is all throat and she has no English. Inigo says Tomas speaks four languages, Tomas says it's five. His face is that wide emoticon of distress. Every day the back of his neck gets browner and browner. The beggingcoins smell of half smoked cigarettes, flecks of burnt tobacco on them, stink of earth and decay and late nights but then so does Carole and Carole is a popstar. Andy doesn't like them, because he is a snob and doesn't want to encourage them like I encouraged the King of the Tramps who ended up shouting FUCK YOU I WAS ONLY DOING IT TO PLEASE YOU ANYWAY in the shop when he was too drunk to serve.

One day he had grippe he told me, Tomas. 'What is wrong with you,' I asked, 'you look awful'. 'Grippe,' his eyes glossy and his skin a weirder colour than usual, his skin waxy, textbook waxy grey. They stayed out though, even though they were sick. I thought maybe they were coming off drugs or were on them or they'd taken something bad or something, I'd never even heard of grippe but it's a funny word and the French root is to snatch whilst the German is flu.

Tommy who plays the guitar out at the front of the Subway – who used to play guitar out at the front of the Co-op – says that they're bad, Tomas and his wife. He came in to tell me, conspiratorially, at the edge of the shop, 'can I have a word, Fee?' that they were Bad People, that he'd seen them at the clinic, that they were heroin addicts, that they weren't to be trusted. But also I think Tommy is a bit racist and territorial – I remember him sitting right next to – right next to – the Romanian Ladies when they were bussed in and out every morning and there being a begging standoff one day. Then that toad Sandro moved the bin over the road in the middle of the night and outside was quiet for a while.

Tommy is very brown and thin and weathered and wiry and handsome, white-blue eyes, and has recently started wearing a thick, white, knitted fisherman's jumper from the overpriced vintage shop. He twangs away at his guitar, an amped up, brassy twang, it's loud and he's good. He's good at a couple of songs and he plays the songs on repeat, Charles reminded me last week – he used to play the same four songs at the Co-op door and drove Charles mad.

Last week he didn't have his guitar and I asked where his guitar was and he said he had forgotten to charge the amp and now he was worried that his kids would draw up in their cars and see him begging, not busking but begging, and he didn't want them to see him begging again and he kept seeing them in his peripheral vision and he would be ashamed if they saw him. He was twitchy and left early. I have not seen him for a while.

I get used to not seeing people for a while. In the wine shop people pause because they've realised they drink too much or they're spending too much or they've told me too much and then I see them months later and they look healthy and are distant because they remember I'm a pusher and a pervasive pusher and I've heard too much.

I see people not walk past the shop anymore, walk on the other side of the street and not look in – Cliff, Graham, Nice smelling Andrew, Joy.

And there's people who always look in, Hobbit John, George, the Florists.

And there's the people I don't know who look at themselves in the window, check themselves out, pout and look seriously at their reflection, making sure everything fits together and they look like themselves.

Ryan says he saw Big Tam the other day and his face was all messed up, but Ryan is an exaggerator and once had a hernia of the imagination. I saw big

Tam passing the shop on one of the rainy evenings and he looked fine to me, he loped-shuffled and looked fat and shouted, Hiya Darlin, through the door to me and I smiled with all my face.

Big Tam is my favourite. He really is big and I'm not sure where he sits, or how he sits, really he is quite fat. I don't know how he would work it because he is so big and where would his legs go? I can't see how the Tam I know would translate into begging but I know he does because he brings in coins to change, different coins from Tomas and wife, smaller denominations – coppers, five pences, twenty pences.

His voice is huge and grinding and frightening, I guess. Sometimes the customers look around alarmed when they hear him. He sounds like he's drunk, like the back of his tongue is swollen, slow and amused, like he's smoked and shouted himself hoarse, Arite Darlin, ye Big Darlin, ye arite Darlin aye? The boys say he calls them pal and Carole's Wee Yin but I'm always Darlin.

From his pockets comes the smash but other things, too, presented on the counter with his great yellow fingers, a green heart shaped button, short lengths of blue bound wire, flat pebbles, a corner of a playing card. One day he pulled out a small, enamelled, hollow golden egg with a stand and blousy pink flowers stretching across it. 'I collect these, darlin' (long pause and soft long look) 'this one's from the charity shop up that way' (not a pause full of meaning but a soft full pause) 'I get them and sometimes I sell them to the jewellers next door' (ha ha ha) 'I've got somethin for you Darlin ah'll bring it in' but he doesn't.

Tomas asks if he can leave his computer behind the counter and then he does, a CPU nestling among the cardboard. We worry that there are drugs in it or it's stolen but really I just think he is leaving his computer with us for a couple of hours. He and his wife are camping in the churchyard at St Mary's. He's taken to sneaking up on me in the shop and he's good at it and Carole never lets on.

He brings me an empty tube for a thirty-year-old Tawny Port. He found a bag on the street with a sporran in it. A sporran and a superhero onesie, a cape, a mask and a glass ship in a bottle.

Grey Skinny Thomas used to be outside the shop every day until he wasn't. Skinny Thomas' face is very rectangular and all of his features are exaggerated but round, his brow, his chin, his nose all growing towards his mouth. He hated the junkies and took 6 sugars in his tea and I could almost make him smile even though he wore this hard scrunched face and didn't say anything to anyone, hardly even acknowledged the cup in his hands let alone the addition of coins into it. He wasn't embarrassed, he just wasn't really there. He was friends with Half a Head and Half a Head freaked me out, he was unpredictable, loose limbed, drunk.

And then one day he wasn't there any more, Skinny Thomas.

Months later I was struggling getting plates and glasses and boxes of bottles out of a car and he shouted over at me from the bus stop across the street, 'Fee! Fee! Fee! Fee!' so pleased not to be sitting and everything growing together but to be stretched up face to the sky, tall, long. What are you doing, I shouted and he shouted, I'm waiting for a bus and we both just smiled at each other from across the road. I shouted, that's great Thomas that's really great and he shouted, I'll see you then. We stood not shouting, stretching, smiling. The sun was setting at the top of the Great Western Road and he got on his bus.

Tomas says self-proclaimed Guru George is Bad People and I asked him why and he just pulled his sad necky face and said he's Bad and nods at the space he left. He says Ryan was a Good Boy and I know that to be incorrect, so I'm not sure that he is a great judge of character. One day after Tomas charges his phone he shows me a photo of his wife and a small boy, his son. He says his son is in care and they want to go back to Romania but they can't get their son back and so they sit collecting money for him. He angrily asks me for a job and I say he doesn't know anything about wine and he says his family has a vineyard and it's all just fermented grapes and there's nothing to know anyway. I say that all the bottles are different and he looks incredulous and says no, how can they all be different?

It is hot and Tomas has a new pair of fluorescent pink trainers that he has taken off and placed neatly beside him. He tells me I shouldn't be riding a bike, and that Coca Cola tastes like sugar and caramel. I tell him he has a way to go with his tasting notes.

FUTURE
CONTINUOUS

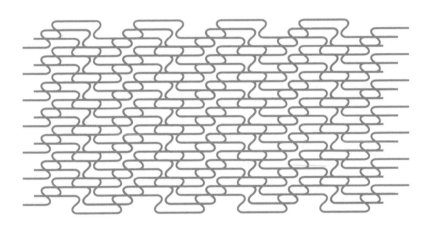

ANJUM
HASAN

In the three months since the cables went mute on the ocean floors and the routers were silenced city by city, I've felt myself become an expert on the subject of loneliness. Watching people from the balcony – office girls, brisk vendors of bruised fruit, tentative retired men, school children who can make a gaiety out of anything, even the drizzle dully dripping off their bobbing umbrellas on a mid-June day – I realise that human features give nothing away. In person, face to face, the soul is easy to exempt from true exposure, it's the simplest thing to hide. So, with this small cage where I pace all afternoon, no links are made, no signals received or sent, the whole world's strung out on a broken line. I can't get across.

The loud squawk of the doorbell. It's my cousin, Deep, whose expression, as always, implies that we ought to have seen it coming. Deep is only eight years older than me but he – with his travelling inspector's job in the Department of Boilers and his lifelong tendency to treat the Net like a contagious disease – is not someone I've ever found even a foothold's worth of common ground with.

'Our government has never trusted it,' he says, settling into my dusty living room. 'All those loud, expensive pro-digital campaigns notwithstanding. Go out into the districts, visit the sub-divisions. They're still squirrelling away everything in string files while one desktop sits like a fat god in the centre, which everyone pays obeisance to but carefully skirts.'

He gives me smug little smiles of vindication and I, so ill with the pangs of separation, don't even try to fend off his departmental small talk. I just sit there twitching softly from the seizures of cyber withdrawal, one eye on my machine just in case, by some man-made miracle, the networks have come life again.

My parents have been calling Deep whenever they can get across on the overworked lines. He is to take me in hand, advise me, urge resilience on me. I must cross the road, buy myself some bread or milk, pay for it with my last notes and coins, learn the first, imbecilic steps again. And then, once I have regained apparently human form, I could become a pen-pusher, join the new offices that are springing up all over the place. I lost my job when the Net broke, as did my house-mate. Saira sat around with me for some time – we played Forty Thieves all day, the pair of decks borrowed from our equally listless neighbour, the frayed cardboard feeling strange between our fingers, and ate Nutella sandwiches and instant noodles to save on grocery bills. We bought the newspapers and tried to figure out when things would be up again. Then she said her parents had had enough, and she took off, back to the mid-sized, middling town she'd come from. She called the other day to tell me she is trying to grow button mushrooms out of crates on her terrace, and that there might be a killing to be made on button mushrooms. Saira, start-up princess, part-mistress of a company that sharpened the edge of cutting-edge, now trying to be a kitchen farmer. But not me. I continue to stay here and dodge my landlady. She is on the floor below me in this duplex, alone and largely unimpaired by the calamity. She can no longer see the faces of her grandchildren on her tablet every night as they lisp in American accents, eating their breakfast cereal and playing their demonic video games, but she has spoken to her son and he's reassured her that everything will be okay.

I know it won't. We managed the rent for a couple of months, but now with Saira gone, my reserves running low, and my brain about to quietly implode with offline provocations that only online can fulfil, I'm no longer quite sure how to carry on living, let alone cover the rent. So I stay in all day and don't answer when Mrs Landlady calls. She's too decrepit to climb the stairs. I let myself out after she's asleep and then I walk the streets the way someone might have in an ancient time – when the nights were dark and solipsism was second nature, when we did not have the world at our fingertips and no one suspected that zeroes and ones could form a language, break up into electromagnetic waves or beams of light, travel a couple or many thousands of miles via satellites or through optical fibres, and then reconfigure themselves into that language of ones and zeroes again to convey messages about the price of petrol, the palette of sunset, the value of love. The bars and the restaurants are doing poorly, the traffic's thin, the hospitals crowded. Some self-proclaimed prophets roaming the streets have already started talking about a post-Net society and the necessity of learning handwriting again. They don't seem to care that I'm still here – sleepless, trembling, nauseous. But still here.

I look at Deep in a daze as he sits there talking about the repair to the steam-lines he's been overseeing somewhere or the other. *My world has died,* I want to cry. But that would be too maudlin for Deep, who never shouts and rarely laughs or weeps, the most phlegmatic of men, the most thick-skinned of bureaucrats, ink in his veins, facts and figures where his heart should be. But I have to make him tea, watery because I'm running out of leaves, and listen to him; I have to nod in dumb protest when he says that this three-decade-long global reliance on the Net was a mere wrinkle in the fabric of history. He is sure that within a couple of years, once the shock has abated, the damage fully assessed and the lost fortunes written off, people will learn alternative skills and create new, more robust technologies.

'We still have everything,' he says. 'The human mind is still what it was. We have land, air, water, and most of our physical infrastructure is still in place – electricity, most importantly. All the hardware for the Net's still untouched, as you know. It's the protocols the masterminds thoroughly scrambled, bless them.'

He clears his throat and smoothes his well-worn trousers. He is forever dressed in some shade of grey and his grey briefcase is always close at hand, resting by the side of his chair as if it held the key to his existence. He opens it now and extracts a flyer.

'Would you like to apply for this? They desperately need officers at the Department of Emergency Communications. Staff to compose and put out statements – when the banks will have cash, when the train and plane bookings will be possible, when the TVs can be hooked up to the old analogue system again.' His eyes flicker anxiously as he holds out the advertisement to me, and I take it but then just sit there slumped in my pyjamas, pleading silently. *But three decades is my whole life.*

When the silence weighs too heavily, he directs a proforma remark or two at me. 'You must meet a doctor. There are medicines for this.' Or, 'We could go for a stroll in the park, the rain is clearing.'

I diffidently study the sheet of paper with its drab and bold-faced officialese, then shut my eyes.

'What'd I have to do?'

'Make calls,' he says on the verge of excitedly, glad I have spoken at last. 'Type letters, queue up at the post office, help the world back to its feet.'

I shake my head. 'Why'd they do this, Deep?'

'The government,' he intones, 'the government has only the concern of the people in mind. They have, and you cannot deny this, they have really risen to the occasion.'

'No, I mean them. The people who brought it down.'

'It was a small cult in the American south.'

'What I want to understand is why people build to destroy.'

But Deep never engages with philosophical questions. He interprets all human sorrow as merely a confusion resulting from incomplete knowledge of material truths. 'A small cult,' he repeats. 'Not well known at all. They waited for a messiah to come and rid the world of fake news, instant messaging and online shopping. When no-one came they took matters into their own hands.'

'No, it was a massive underground movement. They'd recruited the most sophisticated cracksmen, not people who like to let loose local viruses now and then.'

'A spiritual mission – use the Net to bring down the Net and then say goodbye to it forever.'

'Where'd they get the money?'

'No-one knows. Maybe the Vatican. Could even have been a North Korean conspiracy, their revenge on the free world. They say the Net's still working out there. And no arrests so far. They can't seem to find them.'

I think of the grainy pictures I've been seeing in the papers of the abandoned headquarters – a hundred-acre ranch near the Smoky Mountains, laptops full of weapons-grade hacking software and printed literature warning about the impending apocalypse if people didn't get off their smartphones. I run out of words again, again I can only sit there feeling vertigo, that falling without end backwards to a time I don't recognise and cannot adapt to.

Bring me back my love. But I don't know where he is. I have no access to my chats and messages and call logs, I have no photograph saved, no voice recorded, no coordinates noted. I'm not even sure I remember his email address, and we were always on video call, so I don't have his phone number. All I am left with are remembered fragments, the jokey exchanges and shy innuendoes from over the six weeks – or was it eight? – that we knew each other before the great silence fell.

I am erasing myself, cell by cell, with each moment that I miss him and I have missed him now every moment of the past three months. I used to be shocked by how alike we were – not in the matrimonial sense of shared interests, similar backgrounds. It's more as if we'd been created out of the same code, harboured the same reflexes, ran on the same circuitry. He would complete my thoughts for me, I would anticipate his remarks for him. I felt no immediate need to see him and he made no moves to meet me, though we both lived in this city. There was time enough and, besides, we were already together during those late nights when we chatted about the regular things: our compulsive filesharing of movies we had no time to watch, our strange affection for clunky, antique software, our competitive listing of all the apps that no-one had yet thought of, our digital desires, our electronic dreams.

How easily I'd been caught in the grip of a bodiless love with this man: I just had to see his name popping up on the lower right-hand corner of my screen every evening and I was home safe. Times when he didn't come on, I would write him frantic messages and then hold myself back. It was all I could do to stop myself from hitting the Enter key. *Where are you where are you where are you?* He'd return eventually and then I didn't care where he'd been, what he did, who else he was seeing. We were connected. And then the connection snapped. Imagine all the stars in the night sky going out at once and you realising you're really quite alone. Or stepping out of your life to just answer the door, and coming back to find your life's no longer around. *How sickeningly singular, this pain of being forced back onto oneself.*

I blabbered obsessively to Saira, who was more worried about how her disabled father, overworked mother and layabout brother would cope without the money she'd been sending home all these years. So she suggested, to get me off her back, that I put my story down. I do this now, type brokenly on my dead laptop all day. But I don't know how to write this love. He did exist, I know, but the world is conspiring to tell me he didn't. He's not a single one of those apparently living people I watch from my balcony, their true nature masked by the conventions of being in public view. Whereas he and I – no more than two usernames in rapt communion, two unique IP addresses locked into each other – had really grasped what it was to be ourselves.

Deep is saying, 'You do realise Nebular was exactly that? We were under the thumb of a single corporation. That was the undoing of things, I would say. One concern controlling the information superhighway. Its power made it so vulnerable that a single small and devious worm could gulp it down.'

I could at least try and tell Deep about him, ask for a helping hand as I dig my own grave. But Deep might snigger and frown. Or disapprove and lecture. I don't really know Deep. He's the cousin I'd dimly recognise from afar at the random family wedding, the one whose child's birthday party I once went to with a set of neon-coloured laser guns, forgetting the kid was just a year old. And now because there's no-one else my parents know in this city who knows me and can intervene, and because they're puzzled by my obscure disease, unsure about what's eating me, they have enlisted Deep. *Go away. I want the life-giving luminosity of Nebular, not this leaden government with its grim-faced practical measures.*

Instead I say to him, 'I remember a coder telling me once that nobody really knows how this massive creation stays afloat. It's been patched together out of millions of networks and we can tinker with bits of it when they fail but how the whole thing functions is a mystery too complex to understand. Isn't that marvellous? It's like a story then, that's what I figured. You get into a story and are pulled along but no-one, not even its creator, can really tell how all those many small observations, strings of words, sequences of phrases, can make one big coherent whole.'

Deep looks sceptical, then tired. 'I am travelling from tomorrow. Steel plant in the east. Training programme for boiler attendants. I'll drop in again when I'm back. You have some cash left? Enough to eat?'

I can't help letting my relief show; I am out of my chair before he is, and tell him I'll be fine, though I haven't thought about food for days. I stare hard at the thinness of my wrist, at the veins on the back of my hand. This is some new mutation I'm undergoing – nouveau-poor, virtually homeless, literally dying.

Deep glances at me. 'Please don't reject my help,' he declares. 'Do you remember...'

I open the door for him, wait for a parting reminder about keeping in touch with the family, striving to become employable, not giving up on myself.

He says, 'I mean, these circumstances are so difficult for all of us but I am glad that I could...'

'If my landlady hears voices on the landing she might send someone up to harass me,' I say pointedly. He gets out of the house quickly, but his briefcase suddenly seems to have become heavier and he puts it down.

'You,' he says, seemingly with some difficulty, as if pronouncing a foreign word, 'were always my favourite cousin.'

I shrug, but before I can say anything he blurts, 'The money I gave you – please don't ever think of giving it back.'

'I can't right now but I will when I can.' I tap impatiently on the door with my long fingernail, and looking at the chipped polish puts me in mind of the last pic of myself I sent him, and I think of how he might have rendered it screensaver, wallpaper, desktop icon, something, and that he is looking at it now the way I am looking at him now, seared as he is into every chip of my memory.

Deep shakes his head in vehement denial, then launches into a digression. 'Do you remember one time when you were just a child, nine or ten, and

I was helping you with your maths homework? You told me numbers are people – even ones are soft and round, odd ones are hard and grumpy. You said fractions are like trapeze artists and equations are like pole vaulters. You understood very early that numbers can speak.'

I consider my poor, boring cousin and I say nothing. Then I tell him, spelling out the words very slowly and deliberately, 'No, Deep. I don't remember.'

He looks at the scuffed tips of his walking shoes. He gathers up his briefcase as if it were a beloved relative. He turns around and goes down the stairs, and I shut the door before he is halfway gone, then return to the balcony to stare at the many people I cannot bring myself to call out to or touch, like a thirsty hydrophobe crying at the edge of all the planet's water. I wait for the dark like it was an honoured guest. Ten o' clock and I am out in the streets, still in my pyjamas, the hood of my jacket covering my hair, hiding my face, so no-one can tell who's there. I walk long and far. I know what I'm looking for but my stride is hobbled by the fear that the gift I seek is in no place reachable by my finite, human footsteps.

CHIARA ORGANTINI

MARIA VLACHOU

EFFIE SAMARA

SHELAGH WRIGHT

A small group of artists, activists and cultural makers from across Europe with the RESHAPE programme met with Sean Bradley and Effie Samara in Edinburgh Old Town to talk about art, place, belonging, ownership, common ground, community, hopes, storytelling and struggles. Some of them sent postcards from Edinburgh to their friends and family which are reproduced here.

RESHAPE brings together cultural activists to research and develop responses to how art can radically reimagine and renew forms of citizenship and empower us to act through principles of fairness, solidarity, geographic balance and sustainability. It is funded by Creative Europe.

1.

Dear Simone

Next time you hug me I am going to be a bit smoky and sticky as if I am back from a journey across some strange monster's intestine, twisted and dark, misty and bitter... a space where clarity is an illusion or a magical trick, and science is imbued with legend. That's my Edinburgh.

You would love it here, the city is a vortex, full of narrow hallways and shortcuts that climb up to the castle, connecting new town and old town with uncanny associations, a walk that is a speech cut by hiccups, a visual cacophony that glues opposites with pieces of history.

It is all a dance from micro to monumental, a music traveling from an Allegro to an Adagio, my retina was burnt by the grey and the green while feeling sometimes embraced by the grass mountain or caged by concrete walls.

Raise wages not walls the city whispers to me on my way to Calton Hill. There on a magic lookout, former scientific observatory, I realised cannons look like telescopes and sometimes to be able to see and be seen can be a space of vulnerability and aggression.

On which side are we? Are we seen or are we controlling?

Wherever and how far I wish we are always side by side.

Much love from the womb of Scotland,

xxx

Chiara

2.

Whose is the land, my love?
In the beginning was the Word:
Language. Clarity. Truth and untruth.
A declaration of love.
Love of land: Of possession. Of holding and withholding.
Love of carrying.
Carrying in blood, in fluid, in truth, in lullaby.
Carrying.
And miscarrying.
Miscarrying land.
Miscarrying justice.
Miscarrying the secret of womanhood.
The secret of blood, of kinship, the secret of silence – uncoded
Edinburgh, the Athens of the North
Edinburgh, the beloved, my love.
The seat of governments,
The issuer of stamps, infinitely divisible, composing itself of millions of positions, impositions and
Superimpositions.
Whose is Edinburgh, my love?
Crushed, in permanent insurrection against the past.
Dark secret of the French queen's heart and New Kingdom's birthplace.
Seat of philosophers and mathematicians.
Some women too,
Them, mostly unwritten.
Whose is the Land, my love?
In the beginning was the Word, composed according to codes and codicils,
synecdoches and metaphors
A whisper in a child's ear.
A melody
A tympanic resonance: a canon that writes itself and never ceases to inflict discord.
Like a man's endless warring against the quiet workings of the womb.

Against the seeping, weeping, bleeding land.
Whose is the Land, my love?
In the beginning was the Word.
The inveterate counterfeiters' Word.
The Word that comes to haunt our nights with its white truths and its tyranny.
But not for long.
Because, as Word recedes, night falls.
And when night falls,
When the water's skin is cold and awake to mysteries,
When your soft face falls on mine.
When the lids are heavy with the sweet scent of sleep.
Then, my love,
My little love,
Our Edinburgh,
Our Athens in the North,
Is ours.
Again.

Effie Samara

3.

Edinburgh museums have taken me by surprise. Was it like this when I first
visited back in 2006? At the Scottish National Portrait Gallery, I contemplated
the calm faces of 'not-so-calm' people who who did extraordinary things for
the advancement of the Scottish society and Scottish cause. Citizens of foreign
origin, immigrants, are included, they are part. And almost as many women
as men – surprise, surprise indeed...

At the National Museum of Scotland it is again a woman (an arctic explorer)
that opens the Discoveries gallery! More women, Scottish-born or not, are
highlighted in Scotland and the World. They've certainly made an effort...

On the last floor, a guard asked me what I thought of the museum. I gave a
short, polite answer and he must have liked it so much, that he followed me
around, telling me about every object. He had such a lovely Scottish accent,
which means I couldn't understand half of what he was telling me... I was
praying he wouldn't ask me any questions!!!

Oh yes, I wish you were here!

Love
M.

4.

Postcard from Edinburgh to Canon Kenyon Wright (Convenor of the Scottish Constitutional Convention), died 11 January 2017, from his daughter, Shelagh Wright

Dearest Dad

You would so have loved to be in Edinburgh with us this week. The sun was shining (yep, no sideways rain as usual!) and the streets thronged. Too much tartan tat and rose-tinted romantic narratives for my taste but also much that you would be so proud of. A city and a country also looking to its future with clear eyes, sure values and a commitment to community building and social equity in the struggles ahead, for there will be many. I missed you there and I miss you still but know that the ground you always stood on continues to be carefully constructed by others.

With all my love always

Signed

Yer wee un, Shelagh x

Monica Datta trained as an architect in the US, Spain and the UK, including Edinburgh, and currently lives in New York.

Janet Dick worked for more than 30 years in arts education. She has swapped this in recent years for gardening.

Elizabeth Elliott is a lecturer in English Literature at the University of Aberdeen specialising in medieval and Scottish literature.

Lucy Ellmann is a novelist living in Edinburgh. Her first novel, *Sweet Desserts*, won the Guardian Fiction Prize, and her most recent is *Ducks*, Newburyport. Fictionatelier.wordpress.com

Helena Fornells is a poet from Barcelona currently based in Edinburgh. Aside from writing, Helena works as a bookseller and freelance translator.

Kylie Grant is a writer and library assistant who lives and works in Glasgow.

Joyce Guthrie is a community activist living in Edinburgh.

Ellen Hair grew up in Ayrshire. She studied at Stirling University and settled in Edinburgh where she trained and practised as a social worker. She travels frequently.

Anjum Hasan is the author of the novels *The Cosmopolitans, Neti, Neti* and *Lunatic in my Head*, the short story collections *A Day in the Life* and *Difficult Pleasures*, and the book of poems *Street on the Hill*. She lives in Bangalore.

Judith Hertog is an essayist. She grew up in Amsterdam. After living in Israel, Asia and Edinburgh, she has now settled in Vermont where she teaches creative writing. www.judithhertog.com

Astrid Jaekel is a freelance Illustrator and Illustration tutor at Edinburgh College of Art. She grew up in Southern Ireland and Germany, and now lives in Edinburgh.

Kristen Lowman is an actress and a writer of plays and short stories. She was born and raised in Saudi Arabia. She attended the University of Texas, trained at the Webber-Douglas Academy of Dramatic Art in London, and now lives in New York City.

Lesley McAra is Professor of Penology and Director of the Edinburgh Futures Institute at the University of Edinburgh. Glaswegian by birth, she spent most of her childhood in Hull before coming to Edinburgh as a student and falling in love with the city.

Catherine Marshall is an artist, writer and translator currently based in Edinburgh. Born in London, she studied photography at Glasgow School of Art and has lived in different countries and cities including Berlin, which she made her home for a decade.

Lila Matsumoto is a poet and lecturer. She grew up in Japan and the US and studied in Scotland. She currently lives in Nottingham where she teaches creative writing.

Chiara Organtini is a curator and project manager with Centro arti opificio siri (CAOS), a multidisciplinary creative centre in the city of Terni, Italy.

Petra Reid is originally from Lanarkshire. A writer and performance artist, she has lived and worked in Edinburgh for most of her life and is currently developing a cross-disciplinary project on migration and the body.

Suzy Romer was born in Edinburgh. She studied History at St Andrews and worked in the Edinburgh wine trade. Since 2005, she has lived in Logroño in La Rioja, where she writes and teaches English.

Effie Samara is a writer, filmmaker and doctoral researcher in Social Science at the University of Glasgow.

Alice Tarbuck is a writer and academic living in Edinburgh. She is a 2019 Scottish Book Trust New Writers Award recipient and part of Edinburgh-based women's poetry collective, 12.

Rafaela Taylor trained as an architect in Sheffield and in Umeå, northern Sweden. She's now back Edinburgh where she runs a design partnership and is learning to paint.

Maria Vlachou is the executive director of Access Culture based in Portugal.

Phoebe Weller grew up in Fife. She studied English and Anthropology at Glasgow and stayed. She sells wine and talks about cheese.

Shelagh Wright is a cultural activist involved with progressive politics as vice-chair of Compass, and co-convenor of the RESHAPE Group (with Peter Jenkinson).